God's Goodness Always Particular

God's Goodness Always Particular

Second Edition

HERMAN HOEKSEMA

REFORMED
FREE PUBLISHING
ASSOCIATION
Jenison, Michigan

©2015 Reformed Free Publishing Association

All rights reserved

Printed in the United States of America

No part of this publication may be reproduced, stored in a retrieval system, or transmitted in any form or by any means—electronic, mechanical, photocopying, recording, or otherwise—without the prior written permission of the publisher. The only exception is brief quotations in printed reviews

Scripture cited is taken from the King James (Authorized) Version

Cover and interior design by Katherine Lloyd, The DESK

Reformed Free Publishing Association
1894 Georgetown Center Drive
Jenison, Michigan 49428
616-457-5970
www.rfpa.org

ISBN: 978-1-936054-90-9
Ebook ISBN: 978-1-936054-91-6
LCCN: 2015959169

Contents

Preface to the First Edition..7
Foreword..9
Introduction..11

Chapter 1   The Issue..19
Chapter 2   An Untenable Dualism...24
Chapter 3   General Goodness and Our Conception of God 35
Chapter 4   The Exegetical Method..48
Chapter 5   The Concept Goodness of God......................................67
Chapter 6   The Current Teaching of Scripture (1) 80
Chapter 7   The Current Teaching of Scripture (2)............................91
Chapter 8   The Current Teaching of Scripture (3)...........................102
Chapter 9   The Current Teaching of Scripture (4)...........................115
Chapter 10 Temporal Things in the Light of Eternity........................125
Chapter 11 The Triple Cord: Psalm 145:9 135
Chapter 12 The Triple Cord: Acts 14:16–17..................................146
Chapter 13 The Triple Cord: Luke 6:35 156
Chapter 14 Goodness That Leads to Repentance 167
Chapter 15 Grace without Fruits of Righteousness...........................177
Chapter 16 The Particular Longsuffering of God 186
Chapter 17 The General Longsuffering of God................................196
Chapter 18 Conclusion 208

Preface to the First Edition

The following chapters contain a translation of a series of articles that appeared in the *Standard Bearer* that the board of the Reformed Free Publishing Association (RFPA) decided to publish in book form in order to reach more readers than those who read the *Standard Bearer*. Those articles were originally written in the Dutch language, and the board of the RFPA considered it expedient to bring that material also within the reach of those who are not conversant with the Dutch, including especially the younger generation.

Although the author found it tedious to translate his own work, he will consider himself amply rewarded if the purpose of the translation is achieved.

The material is controversial, but the reader will find sufficient positive instruction to make the reading worthwhile.

Let those who are shy of controversy remember that in this world it is impossible to maintain the truth unless one is ready and willing to defend it against gainsayers.

Herman Hoeksema
Grand Rapids, Michigan
November 1939

Foreword

In the mid-1930s Rev. Daniel Zwier, a minister in the Christian Reformed Church, wrote a lengthy series of articles in a Christian Reformed magazine on the subject of God's general goodness. Those articles defended the doctrine of common grace adopted by the Christian Reformed synod of 1924 and attacked the Protestant Reformed Churches' rejection of this error.

Rev. Herman Hoeksema responded with a lengthy series of articles in the *Standard Bearer*, in which he rejected Zwier's presentation of the nature, extent, and objects of God's grace and stated positively the scriptural truth of grace.

In his preface Rev. Hoeksema asked why that material should be published in book form, and then he gave three reasons for doing so.

The first was that a book would have a broader readership than the magazines, and the purpose of an author is obviously to get his book into the hands and minds of as many people as possible.

Second, Hoeksema was very upset with Zwier's constant misrepresentation of the teaching of the Protestant Reformed Churches concerning common grace. He went so far as to assert that Zwier's intention with writing his articles was to destroy the Protestant Reformed Churches.

The third and primary reason was to defend against the error of common or general grace and to develop the truth of God's particular grace.

A similar question can be asked today. Why is the Reformed

Free Publishing Association publishing this book? It is polemical. The content is sharply worded. Motives are judged. Hoeksema says the content is controversial. None of this is popular today in the climate of political correctness. Besides, is this controversy not ancient history? Does it really matter today? If it does matter, why does it matter?

The answer is affirmatively and exactly the same as the three reasons given by Rev. Hoeksema. The value of this book is no different from what it was almost eighty years ago. The reason is that the issue has not changed. At stake is still the doctrine of sovereign grace.

In the defense and development of the true doctrine of grace, the publisher is pleased to present the second edition of this book for the instruction and edification of God's people.

Mark H. Hoeksema

Introduction

In *De Wachter*, the official magazine of the Christian Reformed Church, Rev. Daniel Zwier of Holland, Michigan, wrote a long series of articles under the heading "God's General Goodness." In this series the writer purposed to make clear to his Christian Reformed readers that alongside of and simultaneous with the curse that abides on the ungodly there is a certain goodness, love, favor, grace, loving-kindness, and mercy of God that bless the ungodly in this life until the grave, when for no apparent reason or ground God forsakes them and surrenders them to eternal wrath and desolation. This a brief expression of the main thought of Zwier's conception that he attempted to develop so accurately in his articles that he could not improve it.

The reader understands that Zwier, the editor of the rubric "Dogmatic Topics" (*Dogmatische Onderwerpen*) in *De Wachter*, attempted to defend the doctrine of common grace as the Christian Reformed Church had officially adopted it [in 1924]. He did this under the title "God's General Goodness." For different reasons he preferred the term *goodness* over the terms *general grace* or *common grace*. But his main reason was practical. Zwier has no principal objection against the term *common* or *general grace*. His articles are almost exclusively a defense of the first of the three points adopted in 1924, which declares that apart from the grace, or favor, that God shows only to the elect unto eternal life, there is also a certain favor, or grace, that God bestows on his creatures in general. He therefore treats the subject of common grace.

Considered alone this is a reason to rejoice. That someone in the Christian Reformed Church has sufficient courage to write about the points of difference on account of which that church so wickedly and mercilessly *ejected* us (I use this term emphatically after I read of Zwier's attempt to deny that and will refer to it later) is encouraging and gladdens my heart. I am convinced that discussions of those points of difference will yield positive fruit for the further development of the Reformed truth. For this reason the *Standard Bearer*, which always rejoices in the truth, invited and even challenged the leaders of the Christian Reformed Church to do what their synod had enjoined them to do, that is, to develop more fully the doctrine of common grace. Therefore it is a reason to rejoice that Zwier devoted a series of articles to this subject.

Alas, I must confess that this merely formal fact is the only reason for joy one can find in Zwier's writings. In them there is no positive fruit for the development of the truth. On the contrary, the truth clamors for a reply to his articles.

This is deplorable. Much more profitable it would have been if Zwier had developed the doctrine of common grace, as the synod had enjoined someone to do, and if he had opened new viewpoints and led us in the right direction, in the straight paths of the truth, so that with full confidence we could recommend his articles to the readers of the *Standard Bearer*, as we did the recent writings on the same subject by Prof. Seakle Greydanus and Prof. Klaas Schilder of Kampen.

However, we cannot justify such a recommendation of Zwier's articles. If we would recommend his writings we would serve only the lie regarding the truth and the history of the Protestant Reformed Churches. Zwier's articles do not evince the slightest desire to develop the truth.

The following question cannot be suppressed: why do Zwier's elaborate writings on the subject of common grace not develop the truth to any extent?

Introduction

The answer must be sought by other questions: Why did Zwier write *at this time*? What was his motive for writing?

I am aware that it is difficult to judge motives. But it is also true that with regard to one's motives much can be deduced from the content and style of his writings. One cannot entirely hide his motives for somehow they will be manifested, and sometimes the motives for writing are obvious.

This certainly is true of Zwier's articles. In a few words of introduction he admits that no one ever heeded the injunction of the synod of 1924 to develop the doctrine of common grace more fully. He somewhat deplores this. He thinks that that neglect on the part of the Christian Reformed leaders can be explained somewhat in the light of the circumstances. But he admits their negligence, and he leaves the impression that his purpose is to accomplish this long-neglected task. Therefore, I expected Zwier to realize this purpose in his articles.

But their content is disappointing. Without fear of contradiction and exaggeration, I can state that Zwier is unable to point out how his series further develops the doctrine of common grace. This is one fact that draws the attention of one who peruses his articles.

From this I conclude with certainty that when Zwier started to write he was not motivated by the consciousness of shedding new light on the subject and by the desire to bring that new light before his readers.

Another striking fact is that his articles are permeated with attacks against the Protestant Reformed Churches. He evidently makes these attacks to inform his readers of the horrible, foolish, unscriptural, and un-Reformed character of the thinking of the Protestant Reformed people. They impose their own conceptions on the scriptures and refuse to accept the clear declarations of Holy Writ, while Zwier lives out of a simple faith that unconditionally accepts the scriptures and worships where his faith meets with problems too deep for the intellect to fathom.

From this I conclude that Zwier was largely motivated by the desire to knock out the Protestant Reformed Churches and people before his readers and to picture them as a bad lot of heretics.

I believe too that Zwier was successful to a large extent in his attempt to misrepresent the Protestant Reformed Churches and people before the readers of *De Wachter*, since they do not think for themselves or read the *Standard Bearer* and other publications. Although Zwier corrupted the truth, we do not doubt that many rejoiced in what Zwier wrote. Before the consciousness of many simple souls he no doubt succeeded in branding us as heretics, corrupters of Holy Writ, and destroyers of the church.

One can readily understand this. Zwier has a gift of writing for the common people. He has a ready pen and writes lucidly. He says things pointedly. Long discussions and arguments he avoids. What he writes is easily imbibed. He certainly is the proper man for the task he set himself to perform.

Because common grace is much more pleasing to the flesh, it usually is much easier to make the public believe in it than to have them accept the truth that God's grace is always particular. What is superficial is easily imbibed. One who writes lucidly about things that superficially appear to be true more readily finds an attentive and agreeable reading public than one who inquires concerning the deeper ground and cause of things. Strange though it may seem, Zwier admits that one must remain superficial to maintain the doctrine of common grace: "When we speak of general or common grace, it is indeed true that we remain on the surface of things and consider only visible and temporal things. We do not inquire regarding the ground of things" (God's General Goodness, 26).

We ask, how dare a Reformed man write this?

Zwier answers, "This is permissible because scripture gives us the example." (God's General Goodness, 26).

The scripture is our example in being superficial? Holy Writ, God's revelation, which always shows us all things from the viewpoint of the work of God and his eternal good pleasure, is our example in being satisfied with the surface of things? The scriptures—which reveal what eye has not seen and ear has not heard and could never arise in the heart of man and divert our eyes from visible and temporal things toward the invisible and eternal things—permit us to consider only things that are seen and temporal?

It is not my purpose now to criticize. I intend only to give the reasons for my conviction that Zwier's articles found a ready entrance into the hearts and minds of his readers who are unaccustomed to think for themselves. The reasons are that one who speaks of common grace must remain superficial, and the superficial is easily imbibed by the public. One who separates the temporal from the eternal, the seen things from the unseen things, can easily prove that there is common grace.

Zwier's success with the readers of *De Wachter* must also be attributed to the fact that he can write about us what he pleases, since we do not have the opportunity to defend ourselves before the reading public for which he writes.

He accuses us of many things and writes many ugly and untrue things about us. He repeatedly states that he faithfully read whatever we wrote on this subject in order to leave the impression with his readers that he is thoroughly acquainted with our view of the subject and correctly presents it. But except in a single instance he never quotes us in our own words. He informs his readers regarding our way of thinking and particularly our method of distorting scripture, but he carefully avoids quoting literally from our writings.

In the Netherlands Valentine Hepp was recently criticized for quoting from the works of those whom he attacked without giving any references. Thus those quotations could not be checked. But Zwier's method is worse and is to be condemned more severely than Hepp's method. He at least quoted his opponents; Zwier never (with one exception) gives us the privilege of expressing our views in our own words. He presumes to speak for us. Without proving from our writings and allowing us to speak for ourselves, he repeatedly assures his readers that we proceed from preconceived notions in our interpretations of Holy Writ.

What makes matters worse, it is evident from his occasional admissions that he is only superficially acquainted with our views. He did not investigate our writings carefully and made very little study of the subject. This is evident, for instance, when he confesses that until recently he did not know how we interpret the word "longsuffering" in Romans 9:22. Such ignorance is inexcusable for a critic. More than once we have written about Romans 9:22 and offered our interpretation of it. We replied to Hepp's criticism and interpreted that passage in the book *Van Zonde en Genade* (Sin and grace), written several years ago [by myself and Henry Danhof]. It is evident from Zwier's writings that he is unacquainted with our interpretation of that passage (God's General Goodness, 22).

We certainly are grieved that Zwier presumes to write about our views, criticizes them severely, and exposes us before his readers as heretics, without presenting our views to his readers in our words. Zwier certainly cannot be trusted to be our spokesman. He cannot be objective because of his strong desire to show that we depart from the Reformed truth.

Because the *Standard Bearer* reaches only a limited number of the readers of *De Wachter*, for whom Zwier writes, we have no opportunity to defend ourselves against his unjust accusations before most of his readers. Therefore, they must judge matters on the basis of the one-sided and much distorted information they receive through Zwier's articles.

From all these facts—that Zwier's articles are permeated with attacks on us that grow more bitter as he continues to write, that he presents us to the readers of *De Wachter* as heretics and distorters of Holy Writ who subject plain scriptural teachings to their own

Introduction

preconceived notions and interpret parts of the Bible to suit their dogmatic prejudices and as schismatics who were not cast out by the Christian Reformed Church but willfully severed the bond of fellowship with the church—I conclude that in writing his articles Zwier was mainly motivated by the desire to destroy us.

Still another fact must be considered. Zwier devotes much attention to what Professor Greydanus and Professor Schilder recently wrote about common grace. It can hardly escape notice that Zwier desperately and deliberately attempts to show that he and the Christian Reformed Church agree with the views of these two professors from the Netherlands. Even when Greydanus denies by questions that the doctrine of common grace can be maintained when considered in the light of eternity and the counsel of God, Zwier quickly expresses his agreement.

He emphatically assures his readers that we err when we imagine that we are beginning to receive support in the Netherlands. He warns us that we are clinging to a straw. Evidently Zwier did not want his readers to know that some Reformed leaders in the Netherlands expressed doubt concerning common grace and supported our conception of it. This also helps to explain why Zwier wrote on the subject of God's general goodness.

Zwier's apparent success cannot persuade me to keep silent.

I confess that I read Zwier's articles with indignation. It is difficult to believe that a Reformed man, much less a minister who knows his responsibility before God for everything he writes, has the sad courage to misrepresent the matter so grossly. I admit that it set my blood boiling to read Zwier's repeated boasting of his childlike faith that accepted the teaching of Holy Writ in contrast to our alleged unwillingness to submit to all of the teachings of scripture. I will not hide that I felt offended more than once when Zwier accused us of subjecting our exegesis to our dogmatic preconceptions, especially since he rarely exegetes scripture. But in the end this is an issue not of personal feelings but of the truth.

Although it is true that the truth is not always successful in the world, I am convinced that it will gain the victory.

Although we imagine that we can serve *a certain church* by defending her doctrine regardless of the truth, *the church* can be served only by giving testimony to *the truth*.

This conviction impels me to reply to Zwier.

Chapter 1

The Issue

Intentionally I waited until Zwier finished his series of articles to reply to him.

Although one naturally may be inclined to reply immediately when another openly distorts the truth that is dear to his heart, it is common sense to let the other have his full say. Besides, I was sure that Zwier would be finished somewhat sooner if I did not add the fuel of my criticism to his fire. Even so Zwier elaborated considerably on his subject because he read *De Reformatie* and the *Standard Bearer*. Had I interrupted him, he might have indefinitely stretched his series. Besides, having waited patiently until the end, I am able now to create a little order in the material to be discussed and to arrange it under different headings.

First, it is important clearly to grasp the issue between Zwier and us.

The entire matter of common grace with all its implications is not the subject of our discussion. Zwier wrote only on the subject of God's general goodness, that is, approximately on the matter that was dogmatically expressed in the first point adopted by the Christian Reformed Church in 1924. The subjects of the second and third points—restraint of sin and the civil righteousness of the natural man—are not within the scope of this discussion. Nor will

I touch directly on the heart of the first point, the purely Arminian proposition that God in the preaching of the gospel is gracious to all the hearers. Although this cannot be entirely eliminated from the discussion, and it is inseparably connected with Zwier's conception of God's general goodness, it is not the specific issue at present.

The specific question is the same as it was when the controversy regarding common grace began before 1924: Is there in God a favorable disposition, or attitude, of grace, goodness (*benevolentia*), mercy, and loving-kindness that he manifests to the reprobate ungodly in the things of this life?

That is the issue. The difference between Zwier's view and our view on the issue must be clearly understood. To the question above he and I give opposite answers. Zwier answers affirmatively. I maintain that the truth demands a negative answer.

About our view on the matter, Zwier writes,

> There is no common grace, thus they taught. Grace is only for God's elect people. Toward the world of the nonelect God has only an attitude of hatred. He shows them no single favor, not one whit of goodness, not a bit of mercy. Although the gifts God bestows on the nonelect are good in themselves, he gives the gifts with the express purpose of making the nonelect ripe for destruction, to aggravate their eternal damnation. (God's General Goodness, 2)

Although we would have preferred that Zwier quoted us literally and presented our view in our words rather than in his words, and although the above paragraph does not present our full view concerning the things of this life with respect to the ungodly and God's purpose with them, for the sake of the present argument I admit that he correctly presents our view. In and through the temporal things of this life there proceeds an operation of the displeasure and wrath of God on the reprobate ungodly. God always and continually hates all the workers of iniquity. God's curse is on them and pursues them in all their life and walk. In and through the things of this life—their beings and lives, wealth and possessions, gifts and talents, prosperity and success, rain and sunshine, and the like—God works out their destruction and casts them into eternal desolation. The things of the present time may not be interpreted as mere presents that God in his love and favor bestows on the ungodly for their temporal enjoyment, but they must be considered as means whereby the ungodly are obliged to serve God and whereby God realizes his eternal counsel with respect to all things.

In a later connection Zwier writes,

> The deviating brethren not only repudiated the word, but also the matter itself. Their reply amounted to the following:
>
> We do not find fault with a word, but with the matter itself. According to our conviction there is absolutely no grace that God shows to the nonelect, but also no favor, favorable disposition, goodness, loving-kindness, and long-suffering. God does not manifest the slightest token of these virtues to the reprobate. All these virtues he shows only to his elect.
>
> For the ungodly who are not chosen by God there is only divine and burning wrath. From eternity to eternity he hates them and pronounces his curse on them. In great anger he deals with them and causes all things to be conducive to their destruction. He does, indeed, bestow good gifts on them, gifts that in themselves are good, but these he gives to them with the purpose to aggravate their eternal condemnation, to fatten them for the slaughter. (God's General Goodness, 4)

The terminology is Zwier's not ours. He correctly presents the substance of our view of God's attitude toward the reprobate ungodly. We maintain that the ungodly are never the objects of the favor and love of God, but always and only of his displeasure and great wrath. We maintain this because this is the plain teaching of Holy Writ.

From the words Zwier chooses to present our view to his readers, it is evident that this truth is repulsive to him. He dislikes and repudiates this doctrine.

Zwier's view is the direct opposite of this. He wants to maintain that God in and through the things of this life is *always* good and benevolent to all the ungodly, that he is always merciful to them, that he is favorably disposed to them, that he is full of loving-kindness and tenderheartedness with regard to them, and that he richly and abundantly blesses them.

In his articles Zwier tries to develop and to maintain this view over against our view. Thus the difference between his view and ours can be clearly understood.

He teaches that God in this life always loves all the workers of iniquity. We maintain that God always hates them.

He proposes that God is filled with goodness toward all the ungodly. We hold that he is sorely displeased with them.

He maintains that God bestows all the things of this life on all the reprobate ungodly to bless them and to give them earthly and temporal enjoyment. We hold that even through the things of this world God realizes his counsel and prepares the vessels of wrath for eternal destruction.

We would do Zwier an injustice if we would say no more about his view. After all, Zwier is officially Reformed, even as the synod of his churches was in 1924 when it adopted the three Arminian points. Being officially Reformed, he also allegedly maintains the direct opposites of all the propositions we present as being defended by him. He holds not only that God loves the ungodly always, everywhere, and in all things of this life, but also that he hates them always, everywhere, and in all things. He teaches not only that God's favor is temporally on the wicked, but also that from eternity to eternity his wrath abides on them. His view is that God not only blesses the workers of iniquity through the things of this present time, but that he also curses them through these same things and prepares them for eternal destruction.

Perhaps you say that this is nonsense? You object that these are contradictions that no man can believe. You maintain that a man who holds such contradictory tenets violates the fundamental laws of human logic and talks in riddles.

Zwier replies that these are not real contradictions, but they are contradictory to our poor and imperfect human understanding and logic that cannot be trusted. Although they are illogical, they are not riddles but mysteries that must be accepted with childlike faith. According to him, scripture presents these illogical propositions as the truth.

Here then is another point of difference between Zwier and us.

He maintains not merely that many things far transcend our human understanding, but also that saving faith accepts mutually exclusive propositions that are *contrary to all logic* and that the word of God demands us to accept them. We maintain that this is impossible even for saving faith and that scripture never makes such a demand on faith. The truth may far transcend our comprehension, but it never conflicts with the fundamental laws of logic. If it did, it could not be apprehended. A truth that is contrary to our understanding would elude our grasp.

First I will show that Zwier presents this impossible dualism as the object of his simple faith in scripture; second, that in Zwier's presentation we confront not a manifestation of simple and childlike faith, but two entirely different Zwiers and also two gods; third, that the second (Reformed) Zwier entirely disappears from view and only the first (Arminian) Zwier bitterly opposes our view; fourth, that in the light of scripture the first Zwier is condemned.

Chapter 2

An Untenable Dualism

There are many things that far transcend our finite understanding.

One who denies the existence of realities beyond the scope of our limited comprehension must become an atheist. To assume this position is to deny God, for God is the infinite one, and the finite can never comprehend the Infinite. To be willing to accept as truth and reality only what we are able to fathom and grasp by human reason is rationalism, agnosticism, and atheism.

For a Christian who believes the word of God there must remain many mysteries that do not induce him proudly to deny their reality, but to acknowledge his own smallness and insignificance and the infinite glory and greatness of the living God. When scripture speaks of these mysteries, the Christian experiences no difficulty accepting them.

Many truths of revelation are too high and profound for us to fathom. Think of the truth of the Trinity, the truth that God is one in essence and three in persons. We can gather scriptural data concerning this truth, meditate upon them, arrange them in order, and construe them into a doctrine, but after accomplishing this and formulating the fundamental doctrine of the Trinity, we humbly confess that this does not imply that we have fathomed or comprehended the triune God. Or bring to mind the works of God that cannot be explained from the natural and common order and operation of things as we perceive and experience them in this world, those marvelous works whereby God penetrates through the natural order of the world's history and reveals another, higher order of existence that is to come. That the deaf hear and the blind see and the lame walk, that the sea is divided to let God's people pass through, that the sun and moon are arrested in their courses, that thousands of men, women, and children are fed by a few loaves of bread and a couple of fish, that the dead are raised, and that God dwells in human nature—these and many other works of God mentioned in scripture are different from the objects of our perception and experience and cannot be explained by our natural understanding. But no believer in the word of God ever thinks of denying these truths.

There are also truths whose ultimate unity we cannot perceive. How they can be combined into a harmonic whole we do not understand. How God accomplishes all his good pleasure through his rational moral creatures without for a moment denying or violating their responsibility, we do not fully understand. But no Reformed Christian thinks of denying that God does this. They are mysteries. Although all such things far transcend our comprehension, there is nothing in those things that conflicts with the logic of our minds. When we accept these truths, we do not say yes is no, black is white, and right is wrong.

Such mutually exclusive things that imply contradictions the protagonists of the doctrine of common grace would have us accept. Zwier never grows weary of reminding us that the simplicity of a childlike faith in scripture never reveals itself more clearly than when it accepts contradictory propositions that conflict with our logical minds. Faith in scripture humbly confesses that yea is at the same time nay, that black is also white, that right is also wrong, that love is also hatred, that favor is also wrath, and that blessing is also a curse.

It is remarkable that those who pretend to be Reformed and yet teach the doctrine of common grace seem to need such irregularities and mutually exclusive contradictions that our logical intellects deny. Such contradictions seem to be essential for them so they can maintain their presentation of the truth.

The reason for this need of contradictions is not difficult to discover. These so-called Reformed teachers also desire to speak Arminian language. On the one hand, they profess to be Reformed; on the other, they embrace the Arminian error. But these two completely exclude each other.

This was the reason Prof. William Heyns always spoke of two wills in God. According to one will God earnestly desires the salvation of all men; according to the other he gives life only to the elect. Just as Zwier does, Heyns appealed to clear declarations of scripture, which Zwier said, "One with even a quarter of an ounce of exegetical brains" could readily explain (God's General Goodness, 15). Just as Zwier does, Heyns accused us of rationalism when we maintained that such exegesis conflicts with the organic unity of scripture.

First, I will prove that Zwier demands that the simple Christian faith must accept such mutually exclusive and contradictory propositions. I will quote him as literally as possible and as fully as necessary to prove my point.

He writes,

> And now the miserable human logic rather badly deceives some brethren. They reason as follows: That is impossible. Both cannot be true. If the curse of the Lord is in the house of the ungodly and if he made the ungodly unto the day of evil, he cannot temporally show his favor or goodness, his long-suffering or grace, to that same ungodly man. That is absurd. These two cannot concur in God. (God's General Goodness, 12)

Zwier writes more. He has the sad courage to attempt to persuade his readers that "they [the Protestant Reformed] will not accept that God in his virtues, or attributes, is the incomprehensible one." He is not ashamed to offer his readers the following for them to imbibe: "Their conception of human virtues they attempt to apply to the divine virtues. Human virtues are the criterion whereby they measure divine attributes." He teaches his gullible readers as follows: "They let human logic speak the deciding word about the divine virtues. Instead of reverently listening to all that God reveals in his word concerning his attributes, they determine who and what God must be for the ungodly." If Zwier imagines that in these sentences he wrote the truth, he certainly manifests how little he knows about us, and how unscrupulously he writes about things he does not investigate. He is not in a position to furnish even one iota of proof for what he writes in the above quotations.

But this in passing. We are now dealing with Zwier's dualistic notion, which begins to be revealed in the passages from his articles quoted above. It cannot escape our attention that he writes of "the miserable human logic." By this contemptuous characterization he despises one of the most beautiful and precious gifts of God to man. If we take this expression seriously, and do not consider it Zwier's attempt to impress on his gullible readers that we are influenced by an evil spirit ("miserable human logic"), he denies the possibility of all science, theology, dogmatics, and exegesis; and he also denies the possibility of understanding scripture, for it was inspired by the Spirit of the incarnated Logos and is full of that logic on which he heaps contempt. Note what Zwier offers his readers as being the teaching of the word of God, which simple faith accepts, but which we claim to be impossible of acceptance. What our "miserable human logic" declares to be impossible he impresses on his readers as the truth. On the one hand, the curse of the Lord is in the house of the wicked, that is, this curse abides on him here and now in his present life, in his temporal existence, and on the things he receives in this world. On the other hand, the favor of the Lord is in the house of the wicked, that is, on him in his present life and his temporal existence in all things.

Both of these contradictory and mutually exclusive propositions Zwier would have us accept. Not to accept them he brands as rationalism. To believe both is a mark of humble faith.

He does not deny that these propositions are contradictory and cannot be harmonized with each other. He admits this frankly, but he insists that the scriptures teach these absurdities and that it is characteristic of a humble faith to accept them. He calls this reverence for scripture. We, however, consider this teaching that ascribes such absurdities to Holy Writ very irreverent. He considers the acceptance of these contradictions as a mark of childlike and humble faith, but we do not hesitate to find in it a proof of self-deception. I will not deny that Zwier actually *imagines* that he believes these absurdities, but I deny that he really believes them.

It is easy to demonstrate the impossibility of believing such contradictions.

Note that whoever asserts the first (the curse of the Lord is in the house of the wicked), thereby has already denied the second (the favor and blessing of the Lord is in the house of the wicked).

Is not faith a certain knowledge?

If Zwier affirms with certain knowledge that the curse of the Lord is in the house of the wicked, by that affirmation does he not at the same time state that he does not believe that the blessing of the Lord is in that house at the same moment and in the same sense?

Hence I claim that although Zwier perhaps imagines that his faith is able to accept both propositions, in fact he only deceives himself and his readers. Zwier's self-deception has its source in his refusal to interpret the scriptures in their own light.

That he clings to this impossible dualism to uphold his theory of a general goodness of God, while professing to believe in the Reformed truth, is also evident from the following quotation:

An Untenable Dualism

Let us consider the second argument the deviating brethren usually advance in explaining this passage of scripture.

They ask, does not the Bible teach very clearly in Psalm 73 and Psalm 92 that all the good gifts that the nonelect receive are many means whereby the Lord realizes his eternal and unchangeable counsel of reprobation?

In Psalm 73 Asaph at first stares himself blind on the facts that the godly prosper and the righteous suffer evil in this world. He cannot understand why the ungodly have peace and increase their possessions and power, while he is plagued all the day and his chastisement is there every morning.

But when he enters the sanctuary of God, he beholds these same things in an entirely different light, the light of the counsel of God and his purpose with them all. Now he notices that peace and prosperity are for the ungodly nothing else than slippery places on which God places them so that they fall into eternal destruction.

The same thought is expressed more emphatically in Psalm 92 when it declares that all the wicked spring as the grass and all the workers of iniquity flourish so that they may be destroyed forever. And note here especially the word "that," which denotes the Lord's purpose.

Hence the conclusion is that all the good gifts God bestows on the nonelect are given to them in his wrath and hot anger. (God's General Goodness, 16)

It is evident that Zwier understands this truth perfectly, and he professes to believe it. He continues, "We bow, just as reverently as you do, before the truth presented in Psalm 73 and Psalm 92. We do not detract from it in the least. We also believe that God made the ungodly unto the day of evil and that he puts him on slippery places."

Here we meet with the same contradictory propositions, one of which is a direct denial of the other. Zwier alleges to believe both.

He believes that God gives to the ungodly the things of this life, peace and prosperity, with the avowed purpose of bringing them to eternal destruction in his wrath and displeasure, and that by means of these temporal things he sets them on slippery places, by which they are cast down into destruction. He also believes that God bestows on the ungodly the things of this life—rain and fruitful seasons and gladness of heart—in his favor and with the purpose of doing them good and of blessing them.

If you ask Zwier, how is it possible to teach both? He answers that scripture teaches both. If you inquire further, how can you maintain that the word of God contradicts itself? He answers that he makes no attempt to harmonize these two passages of scripture. He considers it rationalism to attempt to explain scripture in harmony with itself. First he heaped contempt on God's gift of logic to man by speaking of it as wretched human logic, and now he denies its usefulness in the interpretation of the Bible.

Zwier accuses us of not believing this. This we readily admit.

He says, "But we do believe all this." We reply, "No, Zwier, you do not believe this either, for by professing to believe the one, you have already stated that you do not believe the other. You are merely deceiving yourself and others."

Note also the following from Zwier:

> You ask whether it is not true then, as the deviating brethren repeatedly state, that God's loving-kindness in the bestowal of these gifts is only beneficial to his people and that, in spite of all these good gifts, the wrath of God abides on the ungodly?
>
> God is merciful in the proper, full, deep, and rich sense of the word only to his people. Only for them his mercy endures forever.
>
> But this does not alter the fact that the Bible also speaks of a general mercy and loving-kindness of God revealed in

An Untenable Dualism

the bestowal of temporal benefits and blessings even on the unthankful, evil, and unrighteous.

We believe both. (God's General Goodness, 17)

Zwier does not hesitate to write that he also believes what "the deviating brethren" believe. God's loving-kindness revealed in temporal gifts is beneficial only to his people. He tries to qualify the meaning of this statement by speaking of God's mercy "in the proper, full, deep, and rich sense of the word." But these words have no meaning at all in this connection. One surely cannot speak of the mercy and loving-kindness of God in the improper, half, shallow, and poor sense of the word. Zwier cannot intend to teach that in this latter sense the mercy of God is over the ungodly. Rather, we must note that by using these qualifying terms he tacitly and by implication admits that the loving-kindness of the Lord is not at all on the ungodly. Does he not also write that no matter how many good gifts the ungodly receive from the hand of God in this present life, his wrath abides upon them?

But he also believes something else.

This something else denies and contradicts everything he professed to believe. In the bestowal of the temporal things on the ungodly, God is merciful to them. In other words, Zwier would have us believe that although in bestowing the gifts of this present life the Lord is merciful to his people, the elect only, yet in giving these things to the ungodly he is merciful to them also. Although by means of these temporal gifts he curses the ungodly and his wrath abides on them in spite of these gifts, yet he also blesses them through these same temporal gifts, and in them they receive a token of his loving-kindness and grace.

Zwier maintains, "We believe both."

We insist, "You cannot believe both, neither do you, for when you affirm the one you deny the other."

When one says yes with respect to a certain matter, and with regard to the same matter he also says no, he forfeits the right to claim that his testimony be accepted as the truth.

Zwier therefore certainly cannot feel offended when I apply that same wretched human logic to him and his teaching and distinguish between two radically different Zwiers. He must even expect this distinction, for he is aware that we apply that "miserable human logic," which he despises, but we highly value as one of the noblest and most beautiful gifts of God to man and which we, in harmony with the will of God and in profound respect for the word of God, apply to the utmost of our power to the interpretation of scripture not to impose our notions on the holy scriptures (true logic never does this), but to understand the scriptures in their own light (logical light, because it is light of revelation). I say, we apply that logic also to those declarations in scripture in which Zwier finds only irreconcilable contradictions. Therefore, we must have nothing of his impossible dualism. I have too much respect for the word of God to accept that its yea is also nay. But how much more must I apply that same logic to Zwier's reasoning! As soon as I do this, there can be only one possible result: there are two Zwiers, and each one presents us with his own conception of God, the one radically different from and opposing the other.

To offer intelligent criticism of Zwier's teaching it is necessary to remember this.

The one Zwier believes as we do that God is merciful to his people only, that he hates all the ungodly, that his wrath always abides on them, that he made them and prepares them for the day of evil, that even through prosperity and peace in this world he sets them on slippery places, and that he causes them to increase and to flourish with the avowed purpose of destroying them forever. But the other Zwier insists that to the same ungodly, in the same sense and through the same temporal things, God is merciful and full of loving-kindness, that in his favor he gives to the ungodly all the things of this life—rain and sunshine, peace and plenty,

An Untenable Dualism

health and strength, gifts and talents, position and power, wealth and possessions, and fruitful seasons and gladness of heart—and through these means he blesses them in this world. The one Zwier fully agrees with us and admits that there can be no doctrine of common grace when we refuse to be satisfied with the superficial and consider all things in the light of God's eternal counsel—that in the proper and real and full and deep sense God is merciful to his people only. Thereby Zwier condemns the doctrine of the first point of 1924. But the other Zwier casts us out of the synagogue on the basis of this truth he professes to believe!

Let the reader not receive the impression that I am attempting to ridicule.

I can see no other way to criticize Zwier's doctrine as set forth in his articles in *De Wachter* and to distinguish between the truth and the lie in his teaching. If we do not make this distinction and remember it constantly, we run the danger of hopelessly confusing matters. If we do not separate the two Zwiers in our criticism, the one Zwier would always insist that we do him no justice and that he also believes the same things we stress.

Clearly understand that we have no dispute with the one Zwier. Him we do not attack. We want to save him. We would like to extend the hand of fellowship to him as soon as he admits that he is directly opposed to the other Zwier. This other Zwier we would like to destroy with the sword not of human logic, but of the word of God handled by the power of a believing logic.

This is not rationalism.

We do not exalt human reason above the word of God, but entirely subject it to divine revelation.

Nor do we deny that there are many things that far transcend our deepest comprehension. The mystery we gladly accept. However, we do not believe that the word of God contradicts itself, but that it is yea and nay. And wherever it may appear to contradict itself, we believe that sound exegesis cannot and may not rest until it has succeeded in interpreting these passages and bringing them into harmony with the current teaching of Holy Writ.

If we should fail in this attempt with respect to a few passages of the Bible, we would still refuse to build on these passages a doctrine that conflicts with the analogy of faith and of scripture, the continuous teaching of the word of God. Rather we would suspend our judgment regarding the true meaning of these passages, humbly trusting that by sound exegesis they will ultimately prove to be in harmony with the whole of scripture and its fundamental teaching.

According to this principle we hope to proceed.

Chapter 3

General Goodness and Our Conception of God

A word must be said about the conception of God that is implied in the doctrine that God is gracious and merciful to the wicked, the ungodly reprobate, in the things of the present time.

Against us, who deny the doctrine of a general goodness of God that includes the wicked as its objects, our opponents often bring the indictment that our view presupposes a terrible conception of God. It is considered a horrible doctrine that God always and only hates the wicked, that he curses them through the things of the present time, and that he causes all things to work together unto their destruction. It pictures God as a cruel, implacable, and terrible tyrant. This judgment is based on the assumption that God is a God of love, that he is far too merciful to hate the ungodly with constant and eternal hatred. Thus Rev. Johannes Vander Mey wrote in a protest to the consistory of the Eastern Avenue Christian Reformed Church of Grand Rapids in 1924:

> My first and greatest objection concerns the pastor's wrong conception of God. According to him God assumes an attitude of pure hatred and wrath over against the world of the nonelect. Even the gifts God bestows on them serve as punishment and are given to them for that purpose. (2)

After the protestant furnished proof by several quotations from our writings to show that it is actually our doctrine that peace and prosperity and all things of this present life are not blessings for the ungodly, nor are intended by God to be such for them, and that God by these things sets the ungodly on slippery places and casts them down into destruction, Vander Mey wrote, "I consider this a horrible doctrine. I abhor such a conception of God and wish to go on record as such. I will always testify against it. Such a God of hatred is not my God" (3).

The terms Zwier chose to present our view are also adapted to leave the impression with his readers that our conception is unworthy of God.

This objection is sentimental rather than argumentative. It has no value as an objection against our conception of God. That someone "abhors" our conception of God may very well testify against his own theology. It certainly is the scriptural teaching that God is terrible for the ungodly. The fact that one thinks that God is terrible cannot be used as an argument to show that this conception of God is unscriptural. The matter does not concern our sentiments about God, but only God's revelation of himself in his word. Only this determines our theology. Hence the indictment that we present God as terrible is a matter of sentiment and cannot have any weight as an objection against our view.

The objection smacks of Arminianism, even of modernism. That objection has always been lodged against the orthodox conception of God, especially against the Reformed view, and it still is.

Just inquire of any one of the numerous Arminian preachers that fill the pulpits in our country, what his opinion is of the Calvinistic conception of predestination. Usually you will discover that he will not attempt to prove from the word of God that Calvinism is false. But he will answer, "Your God is not my God. A God who sovereignly determines the eternal destiny of men is far too cruel and terrible. God is a God of love to all, and all men have a chance to be saved."

General Goodness and Our Conception of God

The modernist raises a similar objection against the orthodox view of vicarious atonement and contemptuously speaks of "blood-theology."

The fact that our opponents raise this same objection against our view concerning God's attitude over against the ungodly argues against them.

Nevertheless, it is expedient to inquire more closely into the truth of this objection. It is not superfluous to ask, which conception of God is really horrible and unworthy of God as we know him from the scriptures? Which conception of God, ours or that of the protagonists of common grace, conflicts with his virtues, not only of righteousness and holiness, but also of love, mercy, loving-kindness, and long-suffering? Is the conception which teaches that God is filled with wrath and displeasure against the wicked, so that through the things of this present life he prepares them for eternal destruction, to be abhorred and judged unworthy of the God of the scriptures? Or is the conception that teaches his love for the ungodly and his favor to them by means of temporal blessings to be considered cruel and horrible and in conflict with God's nature?

To answer these questions, I will apply the last idea to a few illustrations from history and everyday life. It will help us to see the teachings of Zwier and of those who like him hold to common grace in their true light and to evaluate them correctly. When they speak of God's grace with respect to the ungodly, they usually think of the natural man as being good and noble and performing many good deeds, with common grace improving him and enabling him to do the good. When we thus think of the natural man, it sounds acceptable and proper that God looks on this noble and relatively good natural man in his love and favor and that he blesses him with temporal things, even though he is destined to eternal wrath and destruction. But we must not forget that the scriptures know nothing of a noble and good natural man, this product of common

God's Goodness Always Particular

grace, nor can his picture be found in the Reformed confessions. Nor will you discover this noble natural man in the reality of life. We do not teach that God hates the noble and good, but that he has an attitude of wrath and displeasure and hot anger toward the reprobate ungodly. To bring out sharply the implications of Zwier's view in this matter, I call attention to some biblical illustrations.

Call to mind the illustration of Pharaoh. He was filled with hatred against God's people of Israel. He was bent on their destruction. He oppressed them sorely, so that the cries of the children of Israel arose to the Lord of Sabaoth. Pharaoh murdered the children of the covenant. His avowed purpose was to destroy the people of God.

In doing that and executing his wicked designs, he employed many gifts and talents bestowed on him by God. He possessed the personal gifts of intellect and will and employed them in his designs against the people of God and in their execution. From God he had received his existence and all the means for its sustenance. These gifts, talents, and means he had received in common with all men. In addition, he occupied a position of power and authority in Egypt. Especially through his high position he could oppress the people of God's covenant and aim at their utter destruction. He was king. He was a mighty sovereign, clothed with power to impose his will on others. Against him Israel was powerless and defenseless. Pharaoh had received his power and might from God, for God had raised Pharaoh up and placed him on Egypt's throne. What we must clearly discern is that God gave him all these things *continuously*. God did not bestow all those gifts, talents, power, and authority on that wicked king only at a certain moment, and then subsequently Pharaoh possessed them in himself apart from God. Such is never the case with God's gifts. On the contrary, from moment to moment the king was in God's hand. If for one moment the Most High would have withdrawn his providential hand from that mighty and wicked sovereign, he would have possessed nothing; he would not even have existed anymore. In God, Pharaoh

General Goodness and Our Conception of God

lived and moved and had his being, his gifts and power, his position as king, and his authority. Literally every moment, therefore, the king received from God everything he had.

Zwier admits this.

What is the theory of Zwier and of those who teach common grace? They teach that God continuously bestowed all those gifts and powers on Pharaoh in his favor and great mercy. When that ungodly sovereign with devilish ingenuity contrived schemes to destroy the people of God, first through the mediation of the Egyptian nurses, later directly through the command that all the male children of Israel must be drowned in the river, then according to the theory of common grace, God in his loving-kindness had bestowed the gift of that ingenuity on the wicked king. When Pharaoh abused his power to cause the children of Israel to groan under the burden of heavy labor at the brick kilns, according to Zwier's view, God clothed the king with that power in his great mercy. When the king's mighty hand grabbed the people of God by the throat to choke them to death, God at the same moment showed his loving-kindness to that king by strengthening his wicked hand. When Egypt's mighty sovereign repeatedly hardened his heart to oppose the Most High by refusing to let the people go, God's goodness and loving-kindness to the king furnished the strength of mind and will to that hardening of the heart. When Pharaoh let the people depart and then changed his mind and pursued them with chariots and horses to destroy them, all those means and powers—chariots, horses, the mighty host, and the equipment—were gifts of God's grace to the king.

This is the conception of Zwier and of every one who holds to the theory of common grace applied to the case of wicked Pharaoh and his oppression of the people of God. According this theory, in God's goodness and loving-kindness he bestows on the ungodly the gifts and powers they possess.

We claim that this is a horrible conception of God that conflicts not only with the divine virtues of justice and holiness, but also with the love of God to his people.

Would a father furnish a would-be murderer of his child with the knife to accomplish the foul deed?

Against this view we hold that God gave that power and all those means to Egypt's sovereign not in goodness and loving-kindness, but for the realization of God's divine purpose of revealing his wrath and making known his power. God forbore the king in his wrath until he had served the divine purpose to the very end. Let the reader judge which of these views is unworthy of the Most High and presents us with a conception of God that is contrary to Holy Writ.

I present one more illustration from scripture. The ungodly were gathered around Golgotha. They hated God's Christ, his only begotten Son, his beloved, in whom is all God's good pleasure. They made Christ a prisoner, filled him with reproach, condemned him as an evildoer, mocked him, spit on him, buffeted him, scourged him, pressed the cruel crown of thorns on his brow, and finally nailed him to the accursed tree. And they stood under the cross jeering and scoffing and heaping contempt on the Son of God.

What a mighty display of splendid gifts and powers we behold at the cross! What glorious gifts of God were employed in the execution of that wicked plot that sent the Son of God to his shameful death! Gifts of intellect and will were employed in plotting and conspiring against Jesus of Nazareth, in inventing accusations against him, and in his trial and condemnation. Gifts of power and authority were bestowed on the high priest, the Jewish counsel, and the Roman governor. And powers of brute force were employed to capture the Savior, to bind, buffet, scourge, and maltreat him, and finally to nail him to the cross!

Zwier's teaching is that in his great mercy and goodness over that wicked world God caused his sun to rise the morning of that darkest of days on that ungodly mob that crucified his Son, that in

General Goodness and Our Conception of God

his favor God gave them the minds to conspire against the Lord, the strength in their fists to buffet him, the scourges to lash his back, the power to strike the cruel nails through his hands and feet, and even the pieces of silver to pay the traitor!

Such is the implication of the doctrine of common grace.

There can be no question that God continuously bestowed on those murderers of his holy child Jesus all the gifts and powers they employed in destroying the Lord of glory. Without the continuous operation of God's providence they could not have accomplished their wicked designs.

About this truth there is no difference of opinion.

But it is Zwier's teaching that God in his favor bestowed all those gifts and powers on the murderers of his Son. In Gethsemane, in the palace of the high priest, in the judgment hall of the Roman governor, at the bloody cross, there was a constant manifestation of the goodness and loving-kindness of God toward that wicked world. God's favor strengthened the hand that crucified his Son.

This is a terrible and most horrible conception of God.

We maintain, contrary to this, that God in his providence bestowed on the ungodly world all the powers and means necessary for the execution of their wicked plot, but that he did so not in his favor or grace on the reprobate ungodly, but to the realization of his determined counsel, to the salvation of the elect, and to the destruction of the reprobate who filled the measure of iniquity.

Allow me to call attention to one more scriptural illustration.

Before the second coming of our Lord we expect the kingdom of the antichrist. According to the word of God, that kingdom will be glorious from a worldly viewpoint. That kingdom will be the consummation of all that man can do; it will be filled with prosperity and peace, riches and wealth, and power and honor. Babylon will not only be a great kingdom—mighty in science and art, in commerce and industry, and in worldly pleasures and joy—but it also will be a kingdom in the which there will be no place for the true children of God and those who confess the name of Jesus. They will be subjected to tribulation for Christ's sake; they will not be able to buy or sell; they will be killed with the sword of power and authority. That kingdom will employ its power and greatness against God and the cause of his Son in the world.

Zwier teaches that all those means and all the power of the antichrist are gifts of common grace. He sees in them proof that God is merciful to the ungodly world. The ungodly world that persecutes his church and sheds the blood of his saints God blesses with temporal gifts in his great mercy.

Again we say, this is truly a horrible conception of God.

Contrary to this, we hold the truth that God is greatly displeased with that antichristian world and that even in the bestowal of all the riches and glory it possesses, God executes his wrath and prepares the world for certain and eternal destruction. When the antichristian kingdom will have been realized, we will not speak to the people of God of his great goodness toward the wicked enemies and persecutors of his people, but rather comfort them with the truth that their redemption is nigh and that God is filled with wrath over their enemies.

I will also apply the theory of common grace to a few illustrations from history.

History tells us of that monster of wickedness, Nero, who once occupied the throne of the Roman Empire. That miserable wretch, victim of his own foul and carnal lusts, was suspected of being the incendiary who, to the gratification of his insane lust for pleasure, started the fire that well-nigh laid the proud capital of the empire in ruins. To divert suspicion from himself and to cause the people to believe that the followers of Jesus of Nazareth were guilty of the crime, he subjected them to the most cruel tortures and deaths. Some were crucified; others were sewn in hides of wild beasts and cast to the dogs. It is notorious how that cruel wretch amused himself and the people with the races in the imperial gardens that were

General Goodness and Our Conception of God

illuminated by torches of living Christians put on stakes, covered with a flammable material, and set ablaze.

How many gifts of common grace were required to create that awful spectacle in Nero's gardens! What human power and ability were displayed in those races! What a beauty of nature was represented in those splendid gardens, on which God made his sun to rise and caused his rain to descend! What wicked and cruel ingenuity, which as mere ingenuity was a gift of God, became manifest in the keen suffering of those burning Christians, illuminating the scene of the imperial sports! What power and authority in the sovereign word of Nero that could call into being such a gruesome spectacle! What a gladness of heart was expressed in the shouts and applause of the mob that was gathered to make merry at the groans of God's children!

According to Zwier's theory all those powers and gifts must be viewed as manifestations of the loving and gracious disposition in God toward those ungodly murderers of his people.

It cannot be denied that the terrible spectacles in the gardens of the wicked and cruel emperor could not have been created and continued for a moment if God by his providence had not continuously bestowed his gifts of body and soul, of mind and will, and of power and superiority on the perpetrators of the crimes.

Zwier's contention is that God always blesses all the ungodly in this world with the gifts of the present time.

Again we brand this as a horrible theology, a conception of God that conflicts with everything the word of God reveals concerning the Most High and is contrary to all his glorious virtues. Instead we hold that God in his burning wrath, with great forbearance accompanied by long-suffering over his people, bestowed all those powers on Nero and his ungodly crowd to cast them down into eternal destruction.

We all know of the cruelties perpetrated by the Spanish Inquisition in the age of the Reformation, and of the inhuman forms of torture it invented to bring the sons of the Reformation to a denial of their faith. The faithful confessors of the truth were torn apart limb by limb, their flesh was torn from their bodies by red hot tongs, their tongues were plucked out of their mouths, and slowly they were tortured to death. In all those devilish forms of torture the persecutors employed gifts and talents and means bestowed upon them continuously by the Most High—gifts of God's lovingkindness to them, according to Zwier.

Gifts of God, indeed, we admit, but gifts the Lord of heaven and earth bestowed on them not because he favored them and had an attitude of grace toward them, but because of his good pleasure to use those agents of the devil to try and to glorify his work of grace in his people and to prepare the ungodly instruments for eternal woe.

Let the reader judge which of these two conceptions of God is to be abhorred.

You remark perhaps that I call attention to the most glaring illustrations of iniquity and godlessness. This I admit. I add that I do this intentionally to bring out very sharply the implications of the theory of common grace and its sweet and lovely conception of God.

In the selections of these glaring examples I am perfectly justified, for according to Zwier, this goodness and grace of God to the reprobate ungodly is general. It knows of no exceptions. When we read in Psalm 145:9 that the Lord is good to all, the word "all" according to Zwier's theory includes every man. Always and to all the ungodly reprobate the Lord gives all the things of this life in his great goodness over them. These "all" certainly include Pharaoh, Annas, Caiaphas, Judas, Pilate, the antichrist, Nero, the tormentors of the Spanish Inquisition, and all who ever received gifts of God. When I called attention to a few of many illustrations, I certainly did no injustice to Zwier and to all who hold to the theory of common grace. They will admit everything I wrote in the above paragraphs regarding their view of God's goodness and loving-kindness

General Goodness and Our Conception of God

to the ungodly world.

Although I admit that these illustrations are strong and outstanding, they cannot be considered exceptions that prove the rule. You can peruse all of scripture and you will find many more examples of wickedness as great as those to which I called attention. There you meet with Cain, the fratricide; with Lamech, the proud and vengeful tyrant; with all the ungodly of the prediluvian world concerning whom Enoch prophesied; with carnal and wicked Israel who killed the prophets; with Jeroboam who caused Israel to sin; with Ahab and Jezebel; with Nebuchadnezzar and Antiochus Epiphanes and Herod the great and with many others. From God they all had their lives and beings, their wealth and glory, their names and positions, and all the means whereby they executed all their wicked devices. According to the theory of common grace, in receiving those temporal gifts they were the objects of God's favor and loving-kindness.

Nor do you receive a different impression of the natural man when you turn to the facts of everyday life and experience. You find there not only the coarse and common brawler and profane man, who employs God's gift of speech to curse and abuse the name of the Most High, but also the erudite man of science, who exerts all the power of his intellect to deny and put to naught the word of God and to maintain his own vain philosophy. You meet there with the ungodly, rich employer who sucks the blood out of his poor employees to increase his own wealth, as well as with the ungodly poor who employs brute force in the bitterness of his soul to gain what he considers his share of the world's goods. You have there the sensual debauch who wastes his strength and means to satisfy the lusts of the flesh, as well as the wretched miser who for love of money denies himself and others the barest necessities of life. You meet with the common highway robber who is ready to take your life for a dollar, as well as with the nations of the world who employ their power and ingenuity to invent instruments of murder on a large scale, intended for the destruction of one another. Why mention more? You can multiply these examples by consulting your daily newspapers.

These all continuously receive all their gifts from God. According to Zwier and the theory of common grace, when they employ these gifts in the service of sin and iniquity, they are the objects of God's loving-kindness and tender mercy, and the things of this present life are bestowed upon them in God's favor.

When I say that I utterly abhor and reject such a conception of God as is implied in this theory, I do this not on the ground of humanistic considerations and motives, but on the basis of the word of God.

According to Psalm 73, when Asaph imagined that God favored and blessed the ungodly in bestowing on them peace and prosperity, he had no peace. He did not want it that way. He could not find the theodicy. It was in conflict with everything he knew of God. His soul found rest when he viewed those same dealings of God with the ungodly in a different light—the light that was shed on them from the sanctuary of God, and when in that light he understood that the things of this life that the wicked enjoy are not tokens of God's grace and love to them, but means whereby he sets them on slippery places and casts them into destruction. Zwier's conception of God he abhorred. And do not forget that the author of Psalm 73 was inspired by the Spirit of Christ.

In Psalm 69:22–28 we read:

22. Let their table become a snare before them: and that which should have been for their welfare, let it become a trap.
23. Let their eyes be darkened, that they see not; and make their loins continually to shake.
24. Pour out thine indignation upon them, and let thy wrathful anger take hold of them.

General Goodness and Our Conception of God

25. Let their habitation be desolate; and let none dwell in their tents.
26. For they persecute him whom thou hast smitten; and they talk to the grief of those whom thou hast wounded.
27. Add iniquity unto their iniquity: and let them not come into thy righteousness.
28. Let them be blotted out of the book of the living, and not be written with the righteous.

David directed this prayer against the enemies of God and his anointed, against the reprobate ungodly. Let us guard against the error of the modernists that this psalm belongs to the old dispensation and that it therefore strikes a note that is foreign to the higher standpoint of the New Testament. Ultimately, not David but the Spirit of Christ prayed in Psalm 69. It is plain from Romans 11:7–10 that God heard this prayer. According to scripture it is no less than Christ on the cross who uttered this prayer. Not only is Psalm 69 strongly Messianic, but according to the context of the words quoted, this prayer proceeds directly from the lips of Christ. Plainly, the suffering Messiah is the subject of Psalm 22:1: "They gave me also gall for my meat; and in my thirst they gave me vinegar to drink." The same Messiah continued to speak in the prayer quoted above.

Such is the testimony of scripture.

Terrible, you say? I reply, to be sure but in the good sense. God is, indeed, terrible for the ungodly. This is as it should be, for he is righteous and holy, a consuming fire for those who hate him in time and in eternity.

There is no peace, saith my God, to the wicked! Not even the peace of God's general loving-kindness in the things of the present time, as Zwier would have it. The wrath of God abides on them!

Chapter 4

The Exegetical Method

Zwier writes concerning our explanation of Psalm 145:9: "Yes, esteemed reader, this proof is so utterly weak that for years it was a riddle to me how one with even a quarter of an ounce of exegetical brains could be convinced of it" (God's General Goodness, 15). He writes this in the erroneous imagination that we explained the text to mean that the Lord gives good gifts to all or that the Lord is good to all his elect and his tender mercies are over all things in the realm of redemption. But he fails to mention where he found these interpretations of Psalm 145:9 in any of our writings.

Before I enter into these details and criticize Zwier's exegesis of various texts, I must refer to another, deeper, and more fundamental difference between him and myself, a difference that determines our differing exegetical results. We have a fundamental difference regarding the method of exegesis. This difference explains why my interpretation of certain scriptural passages impresses Zwier as utterly incompetent, so that after years of study he cannot understand how "one with even a quarter of an ounce of exegetical brains" could accept such exegesis. Although I am not acquainted with the standard weight of a normal exegetical brain, I understand that by this somewhat haughty and contemptuous figure of

The Exegetical Method

speech Zwier intends to convey to his readers the opinion that my exegetical work is far below normal. I have attempted to explain how Zwier could arrive at such a contemptuous judgment about my interpretation of the word of God. I came to the conclusion that there is a deep and fundamental difference between his concept and my concept of the proper exegetical method. What I consider exegesis according to the proper method he brands as a distortion of the text to suit my own notions, and what he offers as exegesis of scripture is in my opinion not worthy of the name.

It is imperative, therefore, to give an account of this fundamental difference. As Zwier seems to think, the difference is not that he lets Holy Writ speak for itself, while I impose preconceived dogmatic notions on it. Rather, the difference is that Zwier assumes that interpretation of a text apart from its connection with the current teaching of the Bible is interpretation of scripture, while I am convinced that the word of God is one organic whole that presents the same teaching throughout. Because of this, one can explain a certain text in the Bible without interpreting scripture. The whole of scripture must be considered when one interprets any particular passage, so that every text must be explained according to the rule of scripture (*regula scripturae*), the current teaching of the Bible.

The entire scriptural foundation on which Zwier attempts to build the superstructure of his doctrine of God's general goodness consists of a few individual scriptural passages that superficially appear to support his view. However, his interpretation of them directly opposes not only several other clear texts of the Bible, but also the current teaching of Holy Writ. He is well aware of this conflict and admits it, but he refuses to explain scripture in its own light.

In this chapter I will first demonstrate by a quotation from his articles that Zwier labors according to this method of exegesis. Next I will prove that this method is un-Reformed. Then I will point out the great danger of using this method.

Zwier writes,

> Let us attend now to the second argument the deviating brethren usually adduce in explaining this passage of scripture.
>
> Does not scripture clearly teach us, so they ask, for instance in Psalm 73 and Psalm 92, that all the good gifts the nonelect receive are means whereby the Lord realizes his eternal counsel of reprobation? In Psalm 73 Asaph first stares himself blind on the fact that the ungodly prosper and the righteous suffer in this world. He cannot understand why the ungodly have peace and increase their substance in the world, while he is plagued every morning and chastened the whole day. But when he enters into God's sanctuary, he beholds the same things in a different light, in the light of God's counsel and purpose with all things. He notes that the peace and prosperity of the wicked are only slippery places on the which God sets them so that they fall into eternal destruction.
>
> In Psalm 92 the same thought is more strongly expressed. All the wicked grow as the grass and all the workers of iniquity flourish, *that* they may be destroyed forever. And note the word *that*, which denotes the purpose of the Lord.
>
> Hence they conclude that the Lord bestows all the good gifts on the nonelect in his wrath and great anger. Psalm 145:9 and Acts 14:16–17 must be interpreted in harmony with this. How, then, can one interpret these texts to speak of a favorable disposition of God toward the ungodly?
>
> Our answer to this question is very simple: *Because* scripture *teaches this.*
>
> We do not attempt a rationalistic interpretation of these scriptural passages in harmony with each other. (God's General Goodness, 16)

The Exegetical Method

According to Zwier, we are dealing with series of scriptural passages that are in direct opposition to each other: the one text teaches the exact opposite of the other, and they are mutually exclusive. The one series teaches that in bestowing the things of this life on the ungodly God is merciful to them. The other series teaches that even in the bestowal of these things, God hates the ungodly, is filled with wrath, and purposes to cast them into destruction. We might expect that in reverence to Holy Writ Zwier would reason that "both cannot be true. Scripture cannot teach both, for if it did it would flatly contradict itself. Therefore, one of these series of passages I misunderstand; let me examine my interpretation of both again to come to a correct understanding of the true teaching of the Bible." But this Zwier emphatically refuses to do. He does not even want to put forth the least effort to explain the Bible in its own light. His avowed opinion is that such an attempt would be rationalistic. The result is that he concludes that both teachings are true. God's yea is also nay.

Zwier might have sufficient reason to review his exegesis of the one passage of scripture in the light of the other. Psalm 73 teaches plainly that when Asaph did not view things in their proper light he labored under the illusion that in the things of this present life God is good and gracious to the ungodly. He discovered his mistake when he viewed the same things in the light of God's counsel. How natural it would have been for Zwier to conclude that he labored under the same illusion as the psalmist of old, that he misinterpreted the scriptural passage because he did not view it in the proper light, and that he would have to change his exegesis the moment he studied the passage in the light Asaph received from the sanctuary of God. But in spite of all this, Zwier refuses to interpret scripture in its own light.

When he meets with texts that plainly teach that God's grace is always particular, and his wrath abides on the ungodly in this life, and also finds passages that superficially appear to teach that God's grace is common and general, Zwier puts the texts side by side, in glaring contradiction with each other, and says that both are true.

This method of interpreting the Bible I do not accept. I am deeply convinced that it does not lead to the true word of God, but must lead to a distorted meaning of Holy Writ. Word interpretation is not scriptural interpretation, even though it superficially may appear to be such. Interpretation of individual texts is not interpretation of the word of God, although both for the writer and the reader it may be an easier method to follow. The same is true of many sermons that are praised as clear and convincing. Such sermons explain every word of the texts, but fail to explain the texts in the light of the whole of scripture. Because of this, such sermons are unworthy of the name ministry of the word of God.

I wholeheartedly condemn this method.

How thoroughly un-Reformed the doctrine of common grace is can be gathered from the fact that it can be maintained only on the basis of an exegesis of the Bible that proceeds from this erroneous method of interpretation. When I write *only* on this basis, I assume that Zwier offered us his very best to prove the theory of common grace.

Those who believe and defend the truth of God's absolute predestination have never accepted this method of interpreting the Bible, but have always condemned it as conflicting with the unity of the word of God. The Pelagians, semi-Pelagians, and Arminians have always used this method.

Julian, the arch-opponent of the doctrine of sovereign grace, urged against the doctrine of Augustine the objection that such scriptural passages as 1 Timothy 2:4—which Zwier adduces, following the example of the synod of 1924, to sustain the doctrine of common grace—teach that God wills the salvation of all men and is merciful to all men. But how did the great church father answer the heretic? He spoke of three possible explanations of 1 Timothy 2:4: First, "all" in the text means all of whom God wills to save, for it

The Exegetical Method

is certain that no one can be saved contrary to his will (Augustine, *Enchiridion*, 103). Second, "all" refers to all classes of people not to all individual men. Third, "all" refers to all who will be saved by virtue of the new will infused by God (Augustine, *Contra Julianum*, 22:2).

How did Augustine arrive at those interpretations? Simply by explaining them in the light of the expression in scripture to which he referred frequently, and which Calvin also quoted in a similar connection: God is in the heavens, and he does all his good pleasure. And if God performs everything he willed, he certainly cannot have willed what he does not perform. For that same reason Augustine explained the goodness of God that leads to repentance (Rom. 2:4) as referring only to the elect (A. D. R. Polman, *De Predestinatieleer van Augustinus, Thomas van Aquino en Calvijn* [The doctrine of predestination of Augustine, Thomas Aquinas, and Calvin], 98).

If Zwier had lived in the days of Augustine, he would no doubt have taken sides with the heretic Julian, and would have remarked that "one with even a quarter of an ounce of exegetical brains" would not permit himself to be led astray by such exegesis.

We by far prefer Augustine's method.

John Calvin followed the same method as Augustine. More than once Calvin's opponents confronted him with 1 Timothy 2:4. How did he reply to their objections? He wrote,

> I answer, first, That the mode in which God thus wills is plain from the context; for, Paul connects two things, a will to be saved, and to come to the knowledge of the truth. If by this they will have it to be fixed by the eternal counsel of God that they are to receive the doctrine of salvation, what is meant by Moses in these words, "What nation is there so great, who hath God so nigh unto them?" (Deut. 4:7). How comes it that many nations are deprived of that light of the Gospel which other enjoy? How comes it that the pure knowledge of the doctrine of godliness has

never reached some, and others have scarcely tasted some obscure rudiments of it? It will now be easy to extract the purport of Paul's statement. He had commanded Timothy that prayers should be regularly offered up in the church for kings and princes; but as it seemed somewhat absurd that prayer should be offered up for a class of men who were almost hopeless (all of them being not only aliens from the body of Christ, but doing their utmost to overthrow his kingdom), he adds, that it was acceptable to God, who will have all men to be saved. By this he assuredly means nothing more than that the way of salvation was not shut against any order of men; that, on the contrary, he had manifested his mercy in such a way, that he would have none debarred from it. Other passages do not declare what God has, in his secret judgment, determined with regard to all, but declare that pardon is prepared for all sinners who only turn to seek after it. For if they persist in urging the words, "God hath concluded all in unbelief, that he might have mercy upon all" (Rom. 11:32), I will, on the contrary, urge what is elsewhere written, "Our God is in the heavens: he hath done whatsoever he hath pleased" (Ps. 115:3). We must, therefore, expound *the passage so as to reconcile it with another,* I "will be gracious to whom I will be gracious, and will show mercy on whom I will show mercy (Ex. 33:19). (John Calvin, *Institutes of the Christian Religion,* trans. Henry Beveridge, 3.14.16; emphasis added)

The above is a clear illustration of the method of interpretation Calvin applied to the word of God. First he referred to Deuteronomy 4:7 to show that God sovereignly determines who will come to the knowledge of the truth and who will not receive that knowledge, in order then in the light of that truth to interpret 1 Timothy 2:4. If the opponents still objected that scripture clearly teaches that God will show mercy to all, Calvin replied that such

The Exegetical Method

expressions must be explained in the light of others, such as Psalm 115:3 (often appealed to by Augustine) and Exodus 33:19.

Zwier wants nothing of that method of explaining scripture. He considers it rationalistic. He differs in principle from Calvin. I say *in principle*, for one who applies a wrong method of interpretation to scripture distorts the foundation of the truth and exposes himself to every wind of error. He refuses to compare scripture with scripture and especially to interpret texts that superficially appear to teach common grace in the light of many others that plainly teach the opposite. He insists that he will maintain both. Presently, if he does not relinquish this fatal method, he will be forced by the power of wretched human logic to discard one of the two contradictory propositions and have nothing left but common grace. If he can remain sufficiently inconsistent to avoid this danger, his readers surely will conclude that God's grace is always common.

Allow me to refer to one more illustration from the same paragraph of Calvin's Institutes.

> A stronger objection seems to be founded on the passage in Peter; the Lord is "not willing that any should perish, but that all should come to repentance" (2 Pet. 3:9). But the solution of the difficulty is to be found in the second branch of the sentence, for his will that they should come to repentance *cannot be used in any other sense than that which is uniformly employed* [everywhere in scripture]. Conversion is undoubtedly in the hand of God, whether he designs to convert all can be learned from himself, when he promises that he will give some a heart of flesh, and leave to others a heart of stone (Ezek. 36:26). It is true, that if he were not disposed to receive those who implore his mercy, it could not have been said, "Turn ye unto me, saith the Lord of Hosts, and I will turn unto you, saith the Lord of Hosts (Zech. 1:3); but I hold that no man approaches God unless previously influenced from above. And if repentance were

placed at the will of man, Paul would not say, "If God peradventure will give them repentance" (1 Tim. 2:25). [Calvin, *Institutes of the Christian Religion*, 3.14.16; emphasis added]

Calvin consistently followed the same method of interpretation. He explained the scriptures in their own light and did not hesitate to explain apparently general texts in the light of those that clearly teach God's particular grace.

Do not object that Calvin in the above quotations dealt with saving grace, while Zwier writes about the nonsaving goodness of God. This has nothing to do with the point in question. I am not yet criticizing the content of Zwier's teaching, but only his method of interpreting the Bible. And his method is un-Reformed.

Let Zwier apply the same method to those passages of scripture that refer to saving grace, and his interpretation will certainly be Arminian.

I will refer to a few quotations from Abraham Kuyper and Herman Bavinck.

Bavinck wrote,

> Scripture is the principle of theology. But scripture is no statute book; it is an organic unity. The subject-matter for theology, more especially for dogmatics, is scattered through the whole of scripture. Even as gold out of a mine, so the truth of faith must be delved out of the scriptures with the exertion of all spiritual power.
>
> *With a few proof texts one can do nothing* [emphasis added]. Not on the basis of a few separate texts, but on the Bible in its entirety a dogma must be built; it must evolve organically out of the principles that are present everywhere in scripture. For the doctrine of God, of man, of sin, of Christ, and the like is not to be found merely in a few expressions, but is spread throughout the entire

The Exegetical Method

Bible—not only in a few proof texts but also in sundry figures of speech, parables, ceremonies, and historical narratives. No part of scripture may be neglected. The whole of scripture must prove the whole of the system. Also in theology separatism must be avoided. *A distinguishing mark of many sects is that they proceed from a small part of scripture and leave the rest of it severely alone.* (Herman Bavinck, *Gereformeerde Dogmatiek* [Reformed dogmatics], 1:644–66; emphasis added. All translations from *Gereformeerde Dogmatiek* are mine.)

This is exactly what Zwier does with the proof texts for the so-called general goodness of God. He cannot find a place for this theory in the Reformed system. He quotes a few aphoristic proof texts that conflict with numerous passages of Holy Writ and that he cannot harmonize with such fundamental doctrines as God's righteousness, holiness, wrath against sin, predestination, particular grace, and the cross of Christ. Nowhere do these passages that Zwier interprets as teaching God's loving-kindness toward the reprobate ungodly fit into the current teaching of scripture.

According to Bavinck Reformed theology refuses to acknowledge a few individual texts as a basis for dogma, but with the exertion of all its spiritual powers elicits from scripture the truth of faith. Reformed theology has always considered the doctrine of particular grace as being the current doctrine of scripture, and Reformed theologians never hesitated to interpret other texts that apparently teach general grace in the light of that current doctrine.

But Zwier finds his strength exactly in these separate texts, understanding full well that his entire theory of common grace must fall when they are compared with the rest of scripture. Zwier emphatically refuses to do this. He condemns this method of interpretation as rationalistic. Thereby his method is branded as un-Reformed.

I quote one more passage from Bavinck.

> The theologian must bestow some mental labor on the material he thus obtained. The dogmas are not literally in scripture, but in principle and according to their idea they are conclusions of faith. The doctrines of the Trinity, of the two natures of Christ, of the atonement, of the sacraments, and the like are not based on a single declaration in scripture, but are construed from data scattered throughout scripture. Dogmas are a brief compendium in our language of everything the scriptures teach about the subjects concerned.
>
> Romish and Protestant theologians have always maintained over against various tendencies *that insisted on literal expressions of scripture, the right of dogmatic theology.* According to those theologians, complete justice was done to scripture not by literally quoting a single text, but by reflecting the entire truth comprised in many texts. (Bavinck, *Gereformeerde Dogmatiek*, 1:665–66; emphasis added)

Anyone acquainted with Kuyper's *Encyclopaedie* and his *Dictaten Dogmatiek* knows that I could easily quote similar passages from his pen. But I would rather show how he applied these principles of scriptural interpretation. For this purpose I refer to the well-known *Dat De Genade Particulier Is* (Particular grace), the fourth volume of his series *Uit het Woord* (From the word). Kuyper reasoned from some fundamental truths of scripture to prove that the Arminian doctrine of common grace cannot be true and that all scriptural passages that seem to teach common grace must be interpreted in the light of these fundamental truths of scripture. The doctrine of general grace conflicts with scripture's teaching about the deep corruption of man and his total incapability to accept the proffered redemption. It is also contrary to what Holy Writ teaches concerning the unity and veracity of our God. General grace cannot be harmonized with the doctrine of the person of our Redeemer, who was ordained from eternity as the head of his people, nor with his redemption, which was payment for the guilt of sin and the basis of liberation from the power of sin. Therefore redemption must be particular, for if it is not particular it cannot be an atonement for sin (39–67).

> Since it is a matter of complete indifference to us whether our confession of the truth is in harmony with what some people please to think of God; and since it is our sole purpose *to see to it that our confession completely harmonizes with the living God as he really is and exists*, we can and may do nothing except busy ourselves with Holy Writ, which alone knows and says and shows who God is and how he actually is.
>
> On the contrary, if there is in Holy Writ a revelation of positive truth, as we confess with humble gratitude, it is not only my privilege, but also my solemn obligation to attack your presentation concerning the scope of grace so consistently and perseveringly, that it no longer encroaches on all that is revealed to us in those holy records concerning the *essence* of the Supreme Being. (Abraham Kuyper, *Dat De Genade Particulier Is* 54; emphasis added; all translations from *Dat De Genade Particulier Is* are mine.)

According to Kuyper the scope of grace must be determined by what the scriptures teach concerning the essence of God. He compared scripture with scripture.

According to Zwier that is rationalism.

In opposition to those who wanted to prove the doctrine of general grace from the words "he died for all" in 2 Corinthians 5:15, Kuyper wrote,

> The more limited allegation [that "he died for all" refers to all baptized people] cannot be maintained. For although every member of the church of Christ, be it only externally,

> will be judged by the death of the Lord and by the holiness of his atoning blood. Although the blood of the Son of God concerns such a one, if he does not repent, so truly he will perish as an apostate and a hypocrite. Yet we may not conclude that the apostle of Christ presented the intention of Christ's death as being beneficial for such a one personally. The very fact that the apostle addresses the entire church as elect proves without a doubt that his epistle is directed to the congregation in its ideal character, that is, the letter is addressed exclusively to all and everyone who essentially and as living members belong to the church, without considering in the least with the counterfeit, false, and unsanctified elements that adhere to her, wear her uniform, and present themselves as belonging to her. (Kuyper, *Dat De Genade Particulier Is*, 210–11)

Kuyper explained the apparently general expression "he died for all" in the light of the particular expression in 2 Corinthians 1:1: "Paul an apostle of Jesus Christ by the will of God, and Timothy our brother, unto the church of God which is at Corinth, with all the saints which are in all Achaia."

A clear illustration of the application of this method of interpreting scripture is found in Kuyper's explanation of Romans 5:18, "By the righteousness of one the free gift came upon all men unto justification of life," in the light of verse 21: "That as sin hath reigned unto death, even so might grace reign through righteousness unto eternal life by Jesus Christ our Lord."

> For most people the weightiest objection against the doctrine of particular grace appears to be what Paul wrote in Romans 5:18. There we read clearly in words that seem to allow only one interpretation: "As by the offence of one, judgment came upon all men unto condemnation; even so by the righteousness of one the free gift came upon all men

unto justification of life." We do not deny that the expression "upon all men" is sufficiently emphatic and striking to mislead the best men and even to cause confusion for those of strong convictions who quote it according to the mere sound of words.

Yet by a careful study of the context of this passage, there can be no doubt that this confusion and hesitancy must gradually be replaced by the most positive conviction that sound exegesis does not permit the application of "upon all men" to all men who have been born.

To make this clear to our readers we first call their attention to the closing verse of Romans 5, where sin and grace are again contrasted from the viewpoint of their fruit. There it says that sin results in death and that grace is the mother of life. But how is the operation of both represented? Do we read that sin *attempts* to bring death and that grace *tries* to work life? Not in the least.

On the contrary, if the verse says that sin irresistibly accomplishes its fatal work, that nothing can oppose it, and that with authority it calls death to appear. To express this emphatically and in all its horror the apostle uses the word "reign," to be queen. Sin therefore is mistress, ruler, or queen. She had dominion. Her will could not be resisted. Man was subject unto her. She intended to bring death and no one could oppose that intention. Therefore, it was not that she merely *threatened* death and that after the operation of man's will interposed she either succeeded or failed to bring death. No, with power she caused death to come. As the ruling lady she brought death, and no one could resist her will. Hence all men died.

After the apostle clearly explains this, he declares that the situation is exactly the same regarding grace. Just as sin has dominion, grace appears as ruler and irresistibly executes her will. For thus we read in verse 21: "As sin hath *reigned* unto death, even so might grace *reign*…unto eternal life."

Now this cannot be true if grace, as death, is extended to all men who have been born. If this were the case, we would have to conclude that sin includes all men who have been born and results in the death of them all, and that grace also extends to all men who have been born. However, in reality not all of them, but only a small part of men, inherit life. In that case sin reaches its purpose, but grace fails to reach its purpose. This means that sin succeeded in reigning but grace failed. Instead of ruling over man, grace remained dependent on man's will. This is absurd, for the apostle directly and explicitly establishes the very opposite when he writes, "even so might grace reign." (Kuyper, *Dat De Genade Particulier Is*, 214–15)

From this interpretation of verse 21, Kuyper concluded that the expression "upon all men" in Romans 5:18 cannot refer to all men who have been born.

According to Zwier this method is rationalistic. But it has always been followed by Reformed theologians.

These illustrations can easily be multiplied, but I have abundantly proved that Zwier's exegetical method is not now and never was the method of Reformed people. I am convinced that I am touching on the essence of Zwier's argument. If only he would follow the method of scriptural interpretation always applied by Reformed theologians and relinquish his corrupt method, he would have to acknowledge that his entire argumentation concerning God's general goodness has no basis in scripture.

Allow me to offer one illustration in proof of this last statement. Zwier blindly follows the synod of Kalamazoo in 1924 and offers the following interpretation of Psalm 145:9: "the Lord is good to *all men*."

The Exegetical Method

If we interpret Psalm 145:9 according to the right method, we obtain the following explanation.

First, scripture teaches that God hates the reprobate ungodly, that he is angry with them, that his wrath abides on them, that he causes the things of this present time to work to their destruction, that he sets them on slippery places by means of prosperity and peace, and that he casts the ungodly into eternal desolation. This is not deduced from only a single text, but is the current teaching of scripture. Therefore when we understand Psalm 145:9 in the light of the whole of scripture, the meaning cannot be that God is merciful and good to *every person*.

Second, bearing this current teaching of scripture in mind, we notice at once that the entire psalm speaks of God's grace, goodness, mercy, long-suffering, and great loving-kindness toward his people. Generation upon generation (not of all men, but of his people) shall praise his works and declare his mighty acts. They shall abundantly utter the memory of his great goodness (toward his people) and shall sing of his righteousness. For the Lord is gracious and full of compassion, slow to anger, and of great mercy (vv. 4–8). The Lord upholds all who fall and raises those who are bowed down. He is nigh to those who call on him and will fulfill the desire of those who fear him. He also will hear their cries and save them (vv. 14, 18–19). And if there is any doubt that by this grace, loving-kindness, mercy, and long-suffering of God the psalmist refers to God's people only and not to the reprobate ungodly, note the contrast in verse 20: "The Lord preserveth all them that love him, but all the wicked will he destroy." In all seriousness, would it not be extremely strange if in the midst of all this praise of God's grace toward his people, we would suddenly find a sentence teaching that God is gracious also toward the ungodly, as Zwier would have it? The answer of all sound interpretation is, that cannot be the right explanation of verse 9 when it is viewed in the light of the whole of scripture and of its context.

Third, with all this in mind, we notice two things in verse 9. First, we do not read all men in the text but merely "all." To what does "all" refer? What is its content? May we, as Zwier does, insert here *individual men*, righteous and ungodly? This would conflict with the whole of scripture, the whole psalm, and the text. Second, according to the rule of Hebrew parallelism, the second part of the text explains the first part. The Lord is good to *all*, and his tender mercies are over *all his works*. We explain that the Lord is good to all his works, even as his tender mercies are over all his works. "All" therefore means all creatures in the organic sense, all the works of God, without reference to all the individuals of a certain kind of creatures, as, for instance, men. If we interpret the text thus, it does not conflict with the last part of verse 20: "but all the wicked will he destroy." All kinds of creatures are included in the word "all" in verse 9, but the ungodly are excluded.

This wise, sound, exegetical method will interpret the text. Only thus do we understand the word of God.

Last, I point out that Zwier's exegetical method, which Reformed theologians of every period have always condemned, is also dangerous, first, because it means death for all systematic theology. According to Zwier's method, in which he employs several individual texts to support a certain theory and refuses to explain the texts in the light of the whole of scripture, all true dogmatics becomes impossible. From this perspective one cannot even speak of a current teaching of scripture. Wretched human logic cannot build a system of truth, so we must be satisfied with a concoction prepared by biblical theology that does not care to proceed beyond a literal quotation of scripture. This is the death of the entire Reformed faith and confession. Then there is nothing positive. All unity of view and conception is condemned as rationalistic, and we have nothing left but a few separate and mutually contradictory texts.

Second, Zwier's method is dangerous because the result must be that the doctrine of sovereign grace cannot be maintained. It

The Exegetical Method

was not without good reason that our Reformed fathers always emphatically demanded that certain passages of scripture be interpreted in the light of the whole of the Bible. They did not hesitate to tell the opponents of the doctrine of predestination that individual texts mean nothing to them. The doctrine of sovereign grace stands or falls with the method one applies in the interpretation of scripture. If one follows the method recommended by Zwier, the doctrine of sovereign grace certainly must fall.

In proof of this statement take these words from 1 Timothy 2:4: "[God our Saviour] who will have all men to be saved." Apply Zwier's method to interpret this text, and what do you obtain?

> The text clearly speaks of "all men," and with that term you cannot tamper. I know that scripture also teaches that God is merciful to whom he will be merciful and whom he wills he hardens [Rom. 9:18]. I also wholeheartedly accept this. But I also believe just as wholeheartedly the word of scripture that God wills "all men" to be saved. And "all men" certainly means everybody. You may not attempt to harmonize these two passages with each other, for this would be rationalism. I admit that these two passages directly conflict with each other, and I do not understand how they can be harmonized. But I accept both. God wills only the elect to be saved; he also wills all men to be saved.

The above is the pure application of Zwier's method of scriptural interpretation to a certain series of texts. The reader will admit that I do no injustice to him.

The inevitable result of such an interpretation of scripture will be that one element of the so-called mystery is abandoned and that nothing will remain except the doctrine of general grace and general atonement.

Therefore I pray, Zwier, that you will relinquish this un-Reformed and unscriptural method! For the sake of the seriousness of the truth, confess that you departed from the true way and that you may not so arbitrarily treat the holy word of God! The issue at stake is not dogmatism or maintaining one's church. The issue is the truth, the maintenance and development of the Reformed truth, of which it certainly cannot be said in our day and in our country (and in your churches, Zwier, as you and many others know well) that it flourishes. In that truth I am sincerely interested and earnestly hope and pray that also the Christian Reformed Church, though she cruelly cast us out, may again love and understand and maintain the Reformed truth.

Let Zwier openly return from his dangerous ways on which many of his readers will follow him and depart from the truth. Then possibly there will be hope for the maintenance of the Reformed truth in our country.

Chapter 5

The Concept Goodness of God

Zwier is convinced that serious objections can be made against the term *general grace*. Therefore he attempted to find a better term that expresses the matter more efficiently and completely. One of the reasons Zwier prefers the concept goodness of God is that goodness is a broad concept, the very broadest that can be found in scripture for the subject that Zwier intends to treat.

> Of all the terms that could have been used in the title of my series of articles, the term *goodness* has the broadest meaning. Under this word all the data of scripture can be discussed best…
>
> Scripture speaks of God's mercy over all his creatures. [Under "all creatures" Zwier comprehends the ungodly, and he begs the question and writes this without any proof.] Now, it is self-evident that God's goodness includes his mercy. Mercy is a definite kind of goodness, namely, goodness toward creatures that are in need of help because they suffer and are in misery. [Zwier proceeds from a specific idea of goodness, that of *benevolentia* [the will to bless and make happy.]

All goodness is not mercy, but all mercy is surely goodness. Goodness, therefore, is the broader concept under which we can also discuss mercy...

Scripture speaks of God's long-suffering over the ungodly. [He writes this also without proof.] Without further argumentation it is clear that the goodness of God includes his long-suffering. Long-suffering is a special kind of goodness—goodness toward creatures that have long and severely provoked the Lord to anger. [Again it is clear that Zwier proceeds from a limited conception of goodness, that of *benevolentia*].

Thus it is also with respect to the grace of God.

Reformed dogmatics is accustomed, and rightly so, to discuss this virtue of God under the heading of his goodness, or love...God's goodness and love are so intimately related that it is difficult to distinguish sharply between the two. Usually Reformed theologians mention them in one breath. (God's General Goodness, 11)

With this last remark I cannot agree at all. That goodness and love in God are very closely related is true. But this is true of all God's virtues, for they are all one in him. On the basis of scripture, I deny that no distinction between goodness and love of God is possible, or even that it would be difficult to make such a distinction.

Concerning God's grace Zwier writes,

It is always very evident that the goodness of God includes his grace. Grace is a specific kind of goodness, namely, a goodness toward creatures that have no right or claim to anything and have made themselves worthy of all evil. [In this definition of grace Zwier blindly follows dogmatical works and catechism books, but the definition can hardly be maintained in the light of scripture. Even though it is true that God's grace appears to us and is received by us, guilty creatures, as forfeited goodness, this does not mean that forfeited goodness properly defines the concept grace. According to scripture Christ is first the object of grace, but the grace that has Christ as its object certainly cannot be forfeited goodness. Besides, God is gracious in himself, apart from any relation to the creature.]

All goodness is not grace, but all grace is certainly goodness. Hence goodness is the broader concept under which we can also discuss grace. (General Goodness of God, 11)

It is evident that Zwier prefers the term *goodness of God* not because he has principal objections against the term *common grace*. He does not want to exclude common grace but to include it. When he speaks of the general goodness of God, his intention is not to express less but more than is implied in general grace. He expands. Under general goodness he comprehends common grace, common mercy, common loving-kindness, and common long-suffering. Zwier, by the choice of the term *goodness* intentionally and consciously generalizes everything. He prefers this term exactly because it is the broadest term he can find.

For this reason we must be very careful when we criticize Zwier on this point. It is not easy to define broad concepts. To accomplish this, one must exert all the power of his wretched human logic. Painstaking study of all the terms used in scripture to express such concepts is necessary. Inquiry must be made, with the aid of lexicons, into the significance of the original words in the Hebrew and Greek. But this is insufficient. Various passages of scripture in which certain terms appear that denote a certain concept from a certain aspect must be examined and interpreted in their contexts and compared with one another, at least the most important ones, before one can attempt to define the concept. Thus the exegete, who by a believing logic approaches and investigates holy scripture, will work. The exegete does not have to labor as one who enters an entirely new field of study, but gratefully he may use definitions in lexicons, commentaries, and dogmatics. But he may not be satisfied with blindly following these auxiliary works. Even the lexicons cannot always be trusted. Especially when there is doubt and differences of opinion concerning a certain concept that appears in scripture, he must compare the definitions in the lexicons with the various passages in scripture in which the term is found, subject the definitions to careful criticism, and reject them or improve them if they do not harmonize with Holy Writ. In this way we develop the truth. This is difficult work, and it becomes increasingly difficult as the concepts become more comprehensive.

Very broad concepts leave considerable room for arbitrariness. In defining a broad concept it is easy to consider only one aspect or one element of it and to disregard all others or to emphasize alternately one or the other aspect as it best suits our purpose. Thus when dealing with broad concepts, we run the danger of letting wretched human logic rather than scripture determine the truth.

How did Zwier arrive at his definition of the goodness of God? How are we to judge that definition? How does he apply his definition?

It is evident that Zwier perused a few Reformed works on dogmatics and searched them for a definition. He discovered among dogmaticians many different opinions concerning this matter. Then at a convenient moment he received a copy of *Credo*, the most recent publication by Hepp, where Zwier found a definition that seemed suitable to him, and he chose it.

Thus does Zwier, who has the questionable courage to make his readers believe that we draw conclusions from our conceptions of human virtues and apply them to the divine attributes; that we measure the divine virtues by the criteria of human virtues; that we let human logic determine what the divine attributes must be; that we determine who and what God must be in relation to the ungodly, instead of listening reverently to everything God reveals in his word; and that we let dogmatics dominate our exegesis (God's General Goodness, 12).

He writes all this without a bit of proof. Worse, he is not ashamed thus to write. He is in a position to know better, because our writings clearly testify to the contrary. When he writes his articles and defines the virtue of God's goodness, he performs no exegetical work, does not turn to scripture at all, but consults a few dogmatics by Reformed theologians, finds a definition in Hepp's paper, and offers it to his readers as the definition that best suits him.

Do not think for a moment that I present him in a wrong light. You can judge for yourselves from what he writes.

> What is the scriptural, not human, conception of the goodness of God? Reformed theologians give various answers to this question. They agree on the essence of the matter, but they give a variety of definitions. One circumscribes the goodness of God in one way and another in a different way.
>
> This cannot cause surprise when we recognize that scripture is full of God's goodness. Dr. Bavinck was right when he said that the holy scripture is an anthem of praise on the theme of the goodness of the Lord. No wonder, therefore, that so many different definitions of God's goodness are given. Each theologian sings his own praise of this virtue of the Lord.
>
> But of all the definitions in the different theological works we consulted, none pleased us so well as the one Dr. Hepp offered a few months ago in his magazine *Credo*: "The goodness of God is the *self-desirability of God*." (God's General Goodness, 12)

In a later article Zwier also says that this definition pleased him so well, but even then he does not at all refer to scripture. He merely states that it appears to him that no other definition expresses so well the truth of the word of God.

How is this definition of God's goodness to be judged? In reality we have no definition here at all, but only another word—

self-desirability—that looks at the goodness of God from a different viewpoint. This word does not describe the goodness of God, but a result of his goodness, the attitude that God assumes and must assume concerning himself *because he is good*. When Hepp says that God's goodness is his self-desirability, I understand him to mean that God is in and to himself desirable, that he can and must desire himself alone, and that he eternally desires himself. This is certainly true, but it merely shows the goodness of God from a different viewpoint, the goodness of God in its absoluteness, without defining goodness. God can and must desire himself alone, because he is *the* good, and he can desire only what is good. This lack in the definition that pleases Zwier best is of great significance with a view to the possibility of applying the concept goodness of God to the attitude he assumes toward the ungodly. This is the issue.

When Zwier attempts to define the broadest concept of the goodness of God to use it for his own purpose, he may not fail to do justice to all of its elements in connection with and in relation to one another. Doing this emphasizes the truth that God's goodness is his attribute according to which he is in himself essentially the implication of all infinite perfections. In this sense the term appears a few times in Holy Writ. Thus the Spirit of the Lord is called the "good" Spirit in Nehemiah 9:20. In the same sense the word must be understood in Psalm 25:8: "Good and upright is the Lord: therefore will he keep sinners in the way." A clear instance of this meaning of the word is in Matthew 19:17: "He said unto him [the rich young ruler], Why callest thou me good? There is none good but one, that is, God." This is also the meaning of the word in Exodus 33:19. The man of God beseeches the Lord to show him his glory, and the Lord answers him that he will make all his goodness pass before him and proclaim the name of the Lord. That name of the Lord is the revelation of all his virtues, the expression of all his perfections. In Hosea 3:5 we read that the children of Israel shall fear the Lord and his goodness in the latter days. It is evident that also here the term refers to God's perfections. But apart from these specific passages that expressly speak of God's goodness in this sense, the whole of scripture plainly teaches that God is the perfection of all virtues, or the implication of all perfections, and in that sense he is the absolute good. He is the holy one, the righteous one, the true, the faithful, the only wise and omnipotent God, as well as the merciful and gracious one, the God who is full of loving-kindness. He is love. He is light, and there is no darkness in him at all. He is the infinitely perfect one, who in himself dwells in an inaccessible light.

About God Bavinck writes the following:

> According to scripture God is the implication of all perfections (*bonitas metaphysica*). All virtues are present in him in the absolute sense. In this absolute sense scripture calls him good only a few times…"No one is good but one, namely, God" (Mark 10:18; Luke 18:19). He is…"perfect" (Matt. 5:48). But whatever virtue the scriptures ascribe to God, they always proceed from the assumption that this virtue belongs to God absolutely. Knowledge, wisdom, power, love, righteousness, and the like are ascribed to him in a unique, that is, a divine sense. His goodness, therefore, is one and the same with his absolute perfection. (Bavinck, *Gereformeerde Dogmatiek*, 2:205)

Zwier indeed chose the broadest concept found in holy scripture when he preferred the concept goodness. However, he had no right to limit the meaning of this concept to grace, loving-kindness, mercy, and the like (*benevolentia*). He should not have even started with these virtues, because the perfections of God's truth and veracity, perfect holiness and righteousness, eternity and immutability, omnipotence, wisdom, faithfulness, and all his other perfections are also comprehended within the scope of the concept of goodness. It is possible to view the goodness of God from the aspect of self-desirability exactly because God is absolutely and uniquely good, that is, he is *the* good because his essence is goodness, and as the triune God—the Father through the Son and in the Spirit—he knows and loves himself eternally. God knows himself as the good, as the eternally and infinitely perfect one. Apart from God there is no good and there can be no good. For this reason God can only desire himself as the only good. All his eternal desire has himself for its object. Himself he eternally seeks and finds; in himself he finds his pleasure. In all his divine life he aims at himself with mind and will and all his divine powers. He is the purpose of all his counsel and good pleasure and of all the works of his hands. When he forms a creature outside of himself, that is, creates him after his image; he seeks himself also in that creature, that is, he seeks the glory of his name and thus realizes in that creature his divine purpose that that creature will taste and acknowledge God as the only good.

When we understand the concept goodness in this sense, we admit that Zwier did not make a bad choice when he selected Hepp's definition: God's goodness is his self-desirability. He might have found a suitable point of departure for the further development of the goodness of God with application to the creature. If only Zwier had not purposed to prove that God is gracious and merciful and good to the ungodly and had not permitted his corrupt dogmatics to dominate his good starting point, all might have been well. When we read article 13 of this series, we fostered for a moment the hope that with his development of God's goodness he would turn in the right direction. He writes a few things that warm a Reformed heart.

> When...we speak of God's goodness as his self-desirability, all emphasis falls on the absolutely unique character of God's goodness. It cannot be measured by any human standard, and it far transcends all creaturely goodness. And to mention no more, this definition of God's goodness places on the foreground what must be of supreme importance

for us, namely, God. When we think of God's goodness, we may not first aim at ourselves, but God must be our purpose. God is good in himself, apart from all creatures. He does not need the creature to manifest his goodness. When we hear of God's goodness, we are so easily inclined to think immediately of his disposition to the creature. And, indeed, we may not forget this. Usually this is called the *outgoing* goodness of God. And when we speak of this the questions are, who and what is God for us? But when we understand that God's goodness is his self-desirability, we place on the foreground that God is good in himself apart from the creatures. This idea must precede all others and receive all the emphasis. In dogmatical works this goodness of God is usually denominated his *indwelling* goodness. And when we treat of this the questions are, who and what is God in himself? If God had never made any creatures, it would have been eternally true that God is good, absolutely good, and his goodness endures forever. He does not need the creature to become good, for he is the implication of all good, of all perfections. He desires himself and cannot desire anything else than himself as the highest good.

If only Zwier had constantly remembered this and applied it in his development of the outgoing goodness of God. From the following we received for a moment the impression that he intended to do that:

> When we speak of this we must remember that by the outgoing of God's goodness to the creature the character of this virtue of God does not change. God is the unchangeable, also with respect to his goodness. His goodness before the creation of the world does not essentially differ from his goodness after the creation of the world. His goodness remains essentially the same from eternity to eternity. Also

after creation when his goodness proceeds to the creatures, it still remains essentially self-desirability. In the creature he desires himself and himself only. When he loves the creatures, he loves in them his virtues, works, and gifts. Scripture teaches this when it says that the Lord has wrought all things for his own sake, also the ungodly to the day of evil and that he formed for himself a people to proclaim his praises. In all that God does, in the realms of creation and redemption, he seeks himself as the highest good.

This is purely Reformed language. One who reads this takes courage and is filled with hope that Zwier's development of God's goodness will turn in the right direction. Yet he turns in the wrong direction.

The cause of his turning must be found in his further development of the outgoing goodness of God. In his development Zwier entirely changes the meaning of *goodness*, distorts it, and presents it merely as grace, loving-kindness, mercy, the desire to make happy. Zwier also entirely separates God's goodness from his other perfections, such as truth, veracity, righteousness, and holiness. When Zwier applies all this to the ungodly, he is entirely oblivious that God's goodness is self-desirability and that also in his outgoing goodness God seeks himself. This is abundantly evident from the close of the same article, where Zwier wrote the following:

> When God's goodness goes out to the creature, it manifests itself in different forms according to the nature and disposition of the objects of his goodness, and therefore is called by different names in scripture. If we limit ourselves to three expressions of God's goodness…we find that they are called long-suffering, mercy, and grace. When the creature has made itself worthy of punishment and God does not inflict this punishment in all its fullness at once, but postpones it to a later date for whatever reason, scripture calls this

sparing goodness of the Lord his *long-suffering*. When the creature appears as needy and miserable, and God shows to that creature his favor in helping it in its need, scripture speaks of this commiserating goodness of the Lord as *mercy*. When the creature is viewed as being wholly without rights, so that he can have no claim to anything, and when God shows to that creature, that has merited nothing but evil, his free and sovereign kindness, scripture calls this unmerited goodness of the Lord his *grace*.

Zwier makes all this general. This goodness, grace, mercy, and long-suffering are for all men. God is good and filled with loving-kindness and grace to all without exception. He is favorably inclined to all. It makes no difference whether they are in Christ or outside of him, whether God has known them from eternity as righteous in Christ, or whether he knew them eternally as wicked. I am not losing sight that Zwier distinguishes between God's saving and nonsaving goodness, but in principle this does not change the matter. God is gracious and merciful. In his goodness and loving-kindness he postpones the punishment, helps those in need, and manifests unmerited favor. All this concerns the ungodly and the righteous. There is no difference.

Is it not evident that Zwier makes ample use of the arbitrariness in that broad concept goodness of God? Is it not plain that all of a sudden he forgets that God's goodness is more than grace, mercy, long-suffering, and loving-kindness; that it also includes justice and righteousness, truth and holiness, and all God's perfections; that the goodness of God, even when it proceeds to the creature, is self-desirability and that God seeks himself in that creature? If Zwier had remembered this and applied it, he would have had to say much more. He would have had to say that if the creature is wicked and perverse, and the divine goodness turns against that wicked man in great anger, the goodness of God is called *wrath*. When the creature is a wholly unclean and corrupt sinner, who attacks the glory of God, and the goodness of God makes him miserable and the sinner cannot find peace, the goodness of God is called his *curse*. When the sinner is guilty and worthy of punishment and the goodness of God inflicts temporal and eternal punishments for body and soul on that sinner, the goodness of God is called *justice*. We may not measure the goodness of God by the human standard of goodness. This is exactly what Zwier does. God's wrath and vengeance, God's justice and holiness, God's anger and curse on the ungodly who mock him are also manifestations of his outgoing goodness, of his self-desirability, according to which God seeks himself in the creature, also in the ungodly.

If Zwier had understood this, he would have refrained from prating about a general goodness of God, for then he would have had to distinguish. Then he would have seen that God loves the righteous, is good to the pure of heart, is gracious and merciful and full of loving-kindness to the good, and reveals himself as the good in causing the righteous to taste his favor. In the truth that the righteous taste his grace, God seeks and finds himself as the infinitely good one in that righteous creature. Then Zwier would also have seen that God hates the ungodly, is angry with him, curses him, punishes him with temporal and eternal punishments in body and soul exactly because in that ungodly man he seeks himself as the perfectly good God.

Then Zwier would have found a place for Christ in his treatise on the goodness of God. Now he has no place for Christ. The general goodness of God of which Zwier speaks cannot have any room for him. Others before him have tried to make room for Christ and his cross in the theory of common grace, realizing that it would not do to speak of a Christless grace and favor of God. But this attempt has always failed, and naturally so, for the common or general goodness of God of which also Zwier speaks is divorced from God's righteousness, holiness, and truth. It is no longer self-desirability. The God of Zwier, as he appears in his theory of general goodness, is really not good in the scriptural sense, but only in a humanistic and modernistic sense.

If Zwier had understood what it means that God is really good in the sense of perfect, he would also have perceived that the outgoing goodness of God is revealed in Christ, on whom the Lord emptied all the vials of his good wrath, who completely bore the punishment of his own and fulfilled all righteousness, and who thereby merited grace and eternal life for all whom God has known from eternity.

Then Zwier with us would have concluded that God's goodness is particular.

Chapter 6

The Current Teaching of Scripture (1)

Thus far I have emphasized several truths.

First, I showed that the theory that God is merciful to the ungodly in this present life and gives them all things, gifts and talents and means—which they employ in this world to maintain their ungodly life and conversation in his mercy—leads to an unscriptural and terrible conception of God.

Second, I pointed out that Zwier's exegetical method to support his theory by scripture has never been the method of Reformed theologians and is very detrimental to the maintenance of the Reformed truth. Passages of scripture that appear to be contradictory and that Zwier admits cannot be harmonized, he wants to accept as contradictions without even attempting to explain the Bible in its own light.

Third, it became evident that he distorts the concept goodness of God. He adopts Hepp's definition and explains it as the self-desirability of God. But when he must apply this definition to his subject, he limits the goodness of God to mercy and grace (*benevolentia*), wholly apart from God's ethical perfections of holiness, righteousness, and veracity. It has become clear to the reader that only by this unjustifiable separation is it possible for Zwier to maintain that God's goodness, conceived as *benevolentia*, is also over the ungodly.

The Current Teaching of Scripture (1)

I must now investigate how Zwier interprets certain passages of scripture and on what grounds he rejects our interpretations of them.

Before I do this, however, I must point out the current teaching of scripture on this subject, for this is required by every sound method of scriptural interpretation. Zwier wants nothing of a comparative study of scripture on this point, and he is satisfied with quoting a few texts and offering very superficial interpretations of them. In this he follows the method of the synod of 1924. However, this may not satisfy us. When we claim that the Bible must be interpreted in its own light, we do not mean that two texts of equal value must be interpreted in the light of the other. That would be arbitrary. Rather, we must discover the current teaching of scripture, and if we meet with a few passages that apparently conflict with that teaching, the few passages must be interpreted in the light of the current teaching of scripture.

The current teaching of scripture is that God's goodness is particular. It may seem superfluous to mention this, for it appears that Zwier admits this when he writes the following:

> It cannot surprise us that only relatively few scriptural passages speak of God's goodness, or loving-kindness, in the general sense. The majority of the passages that speak of this attribute of God refer to God's saving goodness. And this, of course, is not general but particular, shown only to the elect unto eternal life. In comparison with these passages, the number of passages that speak of the nonsaving goodness of God is not large. (God's General Goodness, 14)

Here it seems that Zwier admits that the current teaching of scripture is that God's goodness is particular. We are grateful for his concession that he cannot find many texts to support his theory of God's general goodness. This makes my task considerably easier. However, he does not admit that the Bible throughout teaches that God's goodness is particular, but only that it usually speaks of the particular saving goodness of God, and in addition, be it only in a few places, mentions the general nonsaving goodness of God. The contradiction in this he does not see. Later he must admit that scripture also teaches that God is not merciful to the ungodly, but even then he does not hesitate to teach and maintain that God *is* merciful to the ungodly. But here he does not see the contradiction. He only mentions that the current teaching of scripture is that in a saving sense God is merciful to the elect only, and that in a nonsaving sense God is gracious also to the ungodly. And this is not necessarily a contradiction.

That this is his presentation is also evident from his comparison of a similar phenomenon in Holy Writ. He points out that when the Bible speaks of the resurrection of the dead, it usually refers to the glorious resurrection of the righteous and only a few times refers to the resurrection of the ungodly.

> But we do have a few places in which the resurrection of the ungodly is clearly taught. Scripture does not give us much information concerning this resurrection, but the fact as such is well established. Those few places are sufficient for us. And, therefore, we confess that besides the saving resurrection of the people of God unto eternal life there is also a nonsaving resurrection of the ungodly to eternal desolation. The fact that there are relatively only a few texts that speak of the resurrection in this latter sense is no reason for us to doubt it. The word *resurrection* in the one case conveys an infinitely richer and deeper sense than in the other. The resurrection in the real and proper sense of the word only the believers can experience. Thus it is also with the doctrine of God's general goodness.

Zwier continues the comparison. Even as scripture speaks in many places of the glorious resurrection unto life, so it also speaks in many places of the saving goodness of God. Even as in scripture

The Current Teaching of Scripture (1)

the resurrection unto desolation is mentioned only a few times, so also the general goodness of God is supported by relatively few texts. Even as the few passages that speak of the resurrection of the ungodly are sufficient to make us accept this truth and to confess it, so we also believe in the general goodness of God, even though it is mentioned in only a few scriptural passages. The one does not exclude the other.

By a comparison like this the reader is lead astray. Zwier really makes a play on the word *resurrection*. Implicitly he leaves the impression that the resurrection of the ungodly, which he compares with the general goodness of God, is also a blessing. He writes that even as God's goodness in the one case (saving goodness) conveys a much richer and deeper sense than in the other case (general goodness), thus also resurrection in the one case (resurrection of life) has a much richer and deeper sense than in the other (resurrection unto desolation). Yet the one does not exclude the other. Zwier teaches that salvation (resurrection of the righteous) is much richer than damnation (resurrection of the ungodly), that blessing is richer than the curse, that eternal life is richer than eternal death.

Who will not agree with Zwier when he asserts that the doctrine of the resurrection to glory does not exclude the doctrine of the resurrection unto damnation? We all do. There is no difficulty here. There is no semblance of contradiction between these two, nor are there a few scriptural passages that need interpretation in the light of others. But quite different it is with the doctrine of the common, or general, goodness of God. In the illustration of the two resurrections, the one resurrection unto life is for the righteous; the resurrection to desolation is for the ungodly. But the theory of God's general goodness would have us believe that although the goodness and grace of God are particular—only for the righteous—as is admittedly the current teaching of the Bible, yet it is also general for both the righteous and unrighteous. The comparison does not hold. If it were true that scripture teaches one kind of goodness in God for the righteous (saving grace) and another kind of goodness for the unrighteous (nonsaving grace), we would not speak of a glaring contradiction. But the word of God teaches throughout that God hates the ungodly, that he is filled with wrath toward them, that he uses all things to their destruction and curses them. This directly excludes the possibility that it also teaches that with respect to the same ungodly he is also filled with mercy and benevolence. Yet this is what Zwier maintains. Over against this contention it will be my first task to prove that the current doctrine of Holy Writ is not only that God's saving goodness is particular, but also that his goodness in time and eternity is always and only for the righteous and that in no sense can his goodness be said to be over the ungodly. Second, I will show that scripture points the way with respect to the correct interpretation of the few passages that appear to teach a general goodness of God. Third, I will show that these few passages can be interpreted so there is no conflict between their teaching and the current teaching of the Bible.

Scripture throughout teaches that God's goodness is always particular and the ungodly are never its object in time or eternity.

About the psalms Zwier writes the following:

> If you peruse the psalms you will find that when the sacred poets praise God's virtues, they indeed give their attention first and most emphatically to the great deed of the Lord unto the redemption of his people. Nevertheless, they do not lose sight of the goodness and mercy that God manifests in his work of creation and his providence over all the earth and the whole of humanity.

Here again Zwier's language is vague and ambiguous, the same language the synod of 1924 employed in formulating the first point. It is not the question whether God manifests his goodness in all the works of his hands and to all humanity. If this is rightly understood, no one would deny it. God is good to all his creatures; his mercies are over all his works. And there is no conflict between

The Current Teaching of Scripture (1)

his goodness and his saving grace over his people. The whole creation is the object of God's favor and will be liberated in due time and partake in the glory of the children of God (Rom. 8:19–22). Of this the rainbow is a sign and surety. But this is not the question, and Zwier knows quite well that it is not. Why must those who try to defend the theory of common grace forever seek refuge in the use of vague and ambiguous terms? Why not say things sharply and definitely? Zwier means to convey the notion that the psalms speak of God's goodness and mercy over the *ungodly*. Why then speak in general and ambiguous terms of his goodness over all the earth and the whole of humanity? There is only one answer to this question: because the psalms do not contain even a suggestion of a goodness of God toward the unrighteous and wicked. The contrary is true, and this I will prove.

Psalm 1 is the key to the entire collection of psalms. In this psalm we discern clearly the basic note heard in all the psalms: "Blessed is the man that walketh not in the counsel of the ungodly, nor standeth in the way of sinners, nor sitteth in the seat of the scornful" (v. 1). This verse speaks of the blessedness of the righteous in the present time. The righteous man *is* blessed. What is this blessedness? "He shall be like a tree planted by the rivers of water, that bringeth forth his fruit in his season; his leaf also shall not wither, and whatsoever he doeth shall prosper" (v. 3). In contrast with the righteous, "the ungodly are not so; but are like the chaff which the wind driveth away" (v. 4). Why are the righteous blessed and the ungodly cursed? The answer is found in verse 6: "For the Lord knoweth the way of the righteous: but the way of the ungodly shall perish." In his love the Lord knows the way of the righteous, but in his wrath he causes the unrighteous to walk in a way that perishes. Even in this life God's goodness is not over the ungodly.

This is the teaching of the psalms throughout, as I will show by quoting a few passages at random.

Psalm 5:4–6:

4. For thou art not a God that hath pleasure in wickedness: neither shall evil dwell with thee.
5. The foolish shall not stand in thy sight: thou hatest all workers of iniquity.
6. Thou shalt destroy them that speak leasing: the LORD will abhor the bloody and deceitful man.

These verses speak of God's disposition toward the ungodly *in this life*. He *hates* them. He *abhors* them. But Zwier adds that he also loves them and is merciful to them.

Psalm 7:10–16:

10. My defence is of God, which saveth the upright in heart.
11. God judgeth the righteous, and God is angry with the wicked every day.
12. If he turn not, he will whet his sword; he hath bent his bow, and made it ready.
13. He hath also prepared for him the instruments of death; he ordaineth his arrows against the persecutors.
14. Behold, he travaileth with iniquity, and hath conceived mischief and brought forth falsehood.
15. He made a pit, and digged it, and is fallen into the ditch which he made.
16. His mischief shall return upon his own head, and his violent dealings shall come down upon his own pate.

In these verses the attitude of God toward the righteous and toward the wicked is contrasted in clear language. He is angry with the wicked every day, that is, in this life. He is ready to destroy him, for he has prepared for him the instruments of death; he will cause him to perish in his own iniquity. But God's goodness is for the righteous only; he saves the upright in heart.

The Current Teaching of Scripture (1)

Psalm 11:4–7:

4. The LORD is in his holy temple, the LORD's throne is in heaven: his eyes behold, his eyelids try the children of men.
5. The LORD trieth the righteous: but the wicked and him that loveth violence his soul hateth.
6. Upon the wicked he shall rain snares, fire and brimstone, and an horrible tempest: this shall be the portion of their cup.
7. For the righteous LORD loveth righteousness; his countenance doth behold the upright.

This passage also tells us about God's attitude toward the righteous and the wicked in this life. This attitude is presented in sharpest contrast: he tries the righteous, and his countenance beholds the upright; but the wicked his soul hates. The reason for God's twofold attitude must be found in his goodness (goodness in the proper sense of perfection), for he is righteous and loves the righteous.

Psalm 18:25–27:

25. With the merciful thou wilt shew thyself merciful; with an upright man thou wilt shew thyself upright;
26. With the pure thou wilt shew thyself pure; and with the froward thou wilt shew thyself froward.
27. For thou wilt save the afflicted people; but wilt bring down high looks.

The contrast in these verses is clear. The Lord will not show himself merciful with the froward or perverse, and his goodness is not over the man of high looks. The text does not speak of the future, but about God's attitude toward the righteous and the wicked in this life.

Psalm 21:8–12 explains God's attitude over against the ungodly.

8. Thine hand shall find out all thine enemies: thy right hand shall find out those that hate thee.
9. Thou shalt make them as a fiery oven in the time of thine anger: the Lord shall swallow them up in his wrath, and the fire shall devour them.
10. Their fruit shalt thou destroy from the earth, and their seed from among the children of men.
11. For they intended evil against thee: they imagined a mischievous device, which they are not able to perform.
12. Therefore shalt thou make them turn back, when thou shalt make ready thine arrows upon thy strings against the face of them.

Psalm 25:10 instructs us that God's mercy and truth are only for those who fear him: "All the paths of the Lord are mercy and truth unto such as keep his covenant and his testimonies." Zwier would no doubt remark that this passage refers to God's saving mercy and truth. To this we do not object, provided that this saving goodness of the Lord is not limited in Anabaptist fashion to the blessings of regeneration, conversion, going to heaven, and the like. Those who are so fond of the theory of God's common grace in distinction from particular grace are guilty of making this false distinction because they separate the eternal things from the temporal things. But this is impossible. God's goodness, loving-kindness, mercy, and grace always bless and always save in time and eternity. There is no goodness of God that does not save. The goodness of the Lord is over the righteous all their lives, in all their ways, in all the experiences and vicissitudes of this present time, in prosperity and adversity, in health and sickness, and in life and in death. In his mercy he causes all things to work together for good to those who love him. For this reason all the paths of the Lord are mercy and truth to those who keep his covenant, and all the paths of the Lord are wrath and anger to the ungodly. The things of the present time are indeed common, but God's mercy is never common!

The Current Teaching of Scripture (1)

Note also the prayer of the psalmist in Psalm 31:16–23, in which he confesses that God's goodness is over the righteous and his wrath is over the wicked.

16. Make thy face to shine upon thy servant: save me for thy mercies' sake.
17. Let me not be ashamed, O Lord; for I have called upon thee; let the wicked be ashamed and let them be silent in the grave.
18. Let the lying lips be put to silence; which speak grievous things proudly and contemptuously against the righteous.
19. Oh how great is thy goodness which thou hast laid up for them that fear thee; which thou hast wrought for them that trust in thee before the sons of men!
20. Thou shalt hide them in the secret of thy presence from the pride of man; thou shalt keep them secretly in a pavilion from the strife of tongues.
21. Blessed be the Lord: for he hath shewed me his marvellous kindness in a strong city.
22. For I said in my haste, I am cut off from before thine eyes; nevertheless thou heardest the voice of my supplications when I cried unto thee.
23. O love the Lord, all ye his saints: for the Lord preserveth the faithful, and plentifully rewardeth the proud doer.

Note the contrast in Psalm 32:10: "Many sorrows shall be to the wicked: but he that trusteth in the Lord, mercy shall compass him about." Note Psalm 33:18–19 without the contrast: "Behold, the eye of the Lord is upon them that fear him, upon them that hope in his mercy; to deliver their soul from death, and to keep them alive in famine." This is particular, saving mercy, but it is also a mercy that keeps alive in famine. The saving power of this mercy cannot be limited to the eternal future. Hence the people of God sing, "Let thy mercy, O Lord, be upon us, according as we hope in thee" (v. 22).

Psalm 34:8: "O taste and see that the Lord is good: blessed is the man that trusteth in him." He who trusts in the Lord is the only man who can ever taste that the Lord is good. In verses 15–16 the contrast is very sharp. God's goodness is for the righteous only. He turns in wrath against the wicked: "The eyes of the Lord are upon the righteous, and his ears are open unto their cry. The face of the Lord is against them that do evil, to cut off the remembrance of them from the earth."

Psalm 36:7: "How excellent is thy lovingkindness, O God! therefore the children of men put their trust under the shadow of thy wings." Not all the children of men are meant to be the objects of this loving-kindness because not all put their trust in him. If there is any doubt, and some would be inclined to interpret the text in a general sense, let them read what follows: "O continue thy lovingkindness unto them that know thee; and thy righteousness to the upright in heart. Let not the foot of pride come against me, and let not the hand of the wicked remove me. There are the workers of iniquity fallen: they are cast down, and shall not be able to rise" (vv. 10–12).

Do not complain that my refutation of Zwier promises to be a long series of references. Rather, remember that a few proof texts will not suffice to set forth the current teaching of the Bible. It must become clear that scripture throughout teaches that God's goodness is only for the righteous and that the unrighteous are always the objects of his wrath. We will refrain from impatience if we also remember that I am refuting Zwier's theory of general divine goodness and that he repeatedly accused us of rationalism and presented our view as if it were based on a few texts to which we sacrifice the rest of the word of God. This in spite of the glaring fact that in all his twenty-eight articles on this subject he did not adduce half as much proof from the word of God as I offer in this chapter only.

Let us therefore be patient and continue.

Chapter 7

The Current Teaching of Scripture (2)

Let us keep the point in question clearly before our minds. The question is not whether God is good to all his creatures, nor whether his mercy is spread over all the works of his hands. We agree that the earth is full of the goodness of the Lord.

The question is not whether the righteous and the ungodly have in common all the things of this time, such as rain and sunshine. It would be utterly absurd to deny this.

Neither are we discussing whether God's saving grace is particular. Zwier admits that God's saving grace is particular, even though his theory of common grace causes him to stray from the truth on this point. His interpretation of Romans 2:4 is sufficient evidence of this. Nevertheless he agrees with us when we teach that God eternally hates the reprobate ungodly and eternally curses him and eternally casts him into destruction.

But Zwier conceives of a temporal goodness, benevolence, mercy, and grace alongside of God's eternal displeasure, wrath, and anger, of a temporal blessing concomitant with his eternal curse. The ungodly whom God eternally hates he loves in time. The despiser of his name who is the object of God's eternal wrath is temporally the object of his favor. The wicked transgressor of his law whom God eternally curses he blesses for a time in this world. For the present time, strange though seems, this eternal curse and temporal blessing dwell together in the house of the ungodly.

The question is whether the word of God teaches such a goodness, or mercy, of God toward the ungodly and whether the things he receives from God in this world must be regarded as tokens and manifestations of a gracious disposition in the Most High toward the wicked.

In the previous chapter I quoted from scripture to prove that the current teaching of the word of God is that the temporal things God bestows on the ungodly in common with the righteous are not manifestations of God's mercy toward the ungodly. The contrary is true, so that the more the ungodly is enriched with temporal things, the more he becomes the object of God's burning anger. These temporal things are means by which he is called to serve God. The more capital he receives from the Lord, the greater is his responsibility. As he employs all these means in the service of sin, his condemnation is aggravated and he becomes ripe for heavier punishment.

Zwier does not understand this or willfully ignores it. Apparently he likes to emphasize that man is responsible before God, and often he accuses us of denying this. But in reality Zwier does not understand how serious this responsibility of man is. The things of the present time, such as gifts and talents, rain and sunshine, and means and possessions, are not so many Santa Claus presents to man from God for the purpose of man's enjoyment for a time, but they are means with which he must serve and love the Lord his God with all his heart, mind, soul, and strength. Never can the sinner, who uses all these things in his carnal lust and will not glorify God, be thankful and derive real blessings from them; but with them he becomes the object of God's displeasure and curse and of his temporal and eternal punishment, as the Heidelberg Catechism teaches in Lord's Day 4.

The Current Teaching of Scripture (2)

The whole of Psalm 37 describes the contrast between the righteous and the wicked in this life and of God's attitude over against them. In vain you look in this psalm for any support for Zwier's theory. Rather, the entire psalm is one testimony against it. God's people are admonished not to fret because of evildoers, neither to be envious of the workers of iniquity, be they ever so prosperous in the world, but to commit their way to the Lord and to trust that he will bring it to pass. The ungodly may possess an abundance of things in this world, and he may cause the righteous to suffer, but he will surely perish. The Lord *laughs* at him, *for he sees that the day of the ungodly is coming.* Consider what this means with a view to God's disposition toward the wicked in this life. God gives him many gifts, and with them he curses God and persecutes his people, but the Lord laughs at him. Why? The Lord has in mind the day of the wicked, his final destruction (Ps. 37:1–15).

Would not even Zwier hesitate to explain the Lord's laughing at the ungodly as an expression of his loving-kindness?

Therefore, a little that the righteous man has is better than the riches of many wicked. The arms of the wicked will be broken; they will perish and consume away into smoke. But the Lord upholds the righteous. He knows the days of the upright and their inheritance will be forever, and they will never be ashamed, not even in the evil time (Ps. 37:16–20). The righteous is the blessed of the Lord who will inherit the earth. His steps are ordered by the Lord who delights in his way so that even though the righteous may fall, he will never be utterly cast down, for the Lord upholds him with his hand. The Lord never forsakes him, for he is preserved forever. But the ungodly is the cursed of the Lord; he and his seed will be cut off (vv. 22–28). The wicked may be in great power and spread like a green bay tree, but he will pass away and will not be found. But the end of the righteous man is peace; his salvation is of the Lord, who also is his strength in time of trouble. God will deliver the upright and save him, because he trusts in God's name (vv. 35–40).

Psalm 37 speaks of the eternal salvation and blessedness of God's people and of the eternal desolation and destruction of the ungodly; it speaks of saving goodness and of damning wrath. But it does this in such a way that there is no room for a general goodness of God of which the unrighteous and the wicked are the objects in this life. Of a temporal goodness and mercy alongside of eternal wrath and anger this psalm knows absolutely nothing. Time and eternity, the way and the final destination, are inseparably connected. In time and in eternity the ungodly is the cursed of the Lord, although he may wallow in abundance. In time and in eternity the righteous is the blessed of the Lord, although for a time he may walk a way of want and suffering. Such is the plain teaching of this psalm. If Zwier would carefully exegete it, he would certainly and radically change his view.

Psalm 40 is strongly messianic. This means that ultimately the Spirit of Christ speaks of Christ in this sacred song. The Spirit of Christ causes the following prayer to flow from the lips of David:

13. Be pleased, O Lord, to deliver me: O Lord, make haste to help me.
14. Let them be ashamed and confounded together that seek after my soul to destroy it; let them be driven backward and put to shame that wish me evil.
15. Let them be desolate for a reward of their shame that say unto me, Aha, aha.
16. Let all those that seek thee rejoice and be glad in thee: let such as love thy salvation say continually, The Lord be magnified. (vv. 13–16)

Psalm 52:1 says, "Why boasteth thou thyself in mischief, O mighty man? the goodness of God endureth continually." The meaning is not that the goodness of God endures continually toward the mighty boaster who aimed at David's destruction, but that all his evil devices against the man after God's heart must surely

The Current Teaching of Scripture (2)

fail, because David was the object of an enduring divine goodness. God's goodness is particular. The ungodly is not its object. This is plain from what follows in verses 2–8:

2. Thy tongue deviseth mischiefs; like a sharp razor, working deceitfully.
3. Thou lovest evil more than good; and lying rather than to speak righteousness.
4. Thou lovest all devouring words, O thou deceitful tongue.
5. God shall likewise destroy thee forever, he shall take thee away, and pluck thee out of thy dwelling place, and root thee out of the land of the living.
6. The righteous shall see and fear and shall laugh at him.
7. Lo, this is the man that made not God his strength; but trusted in the abundance of his riches, and strengthened himself in his wickedness.
8. But I am like a green olive tree in the house of God: I trust in the mercy of God forever and ever.

Mark also Psalm 57:3: "He shall send from heaven, and save me from the reproach of him that would swallow me up. God shall send forth his mercy and his truth." Do not apply dogmatics to this passage and explain it to refer to David's final and eternal salvation, for that is not the point at all. David will be delivered from the hand of Saul who persecuted him. Note that this deliverance of the righteous from the hand of the wicked and the destruction of the wicked take place when God's mercy and truth, which are inseparable, are sent from heaven.

Study too the prayer of Psalm 58:6–11:

6. Break their teeth, O God, in their mouth: break out the great teeth of the young lions, O LORD.

7. Let them melt away as waters which run continually: when he bendeth his bow to shoot his arrows, let them be as cut in pieces.
8. As a snail which melteth, let every one of them pass away: like the untimely birth of a woman, that they may not see the sun.
9. Before your pots can feel the thorns, he shall take them away as a whirlwind, both living, and in his wrath.
10. The righteous shall rejoice when he seeth the vengeance: he shall wash his feet in the blood of the wicked.
11. So that a man shall say, Verily, there is a reward for the righteous: verily, he is a God that judgeth in the earth.

Let anyone try to find room for the theory of common grace in the following prayer from Psalm 59:

5. Thou therefore, O LORD God of hosts, the God of Israel, awake to visit all the heathen: be not merciful to any wicked transgressor. [In the light of the theory of common grace, such a prayer would be considered wicked.]

11. Slay them not, lest my people forget: scatter them by thy power; and bring them down, O Lord, our shield.
12. For the sin of their mouth and the words of their lips, let them even be taken in their pride: and for cursing and lying which they speak.
13. Consume them in wrath, consume them, that they may not be: and let them know that God ruleth in Jacob unto the ends of the earth.
14. And at evening let them return; and let them make a noise like a dog, and go round about the city.
15. Let them wander up and down for meat, and grudge if they be not satisfied.

The Current Teaching of Scripture (2)

16. But I will sing of thy power; yea, I will sing aloud of thy mercy in the morning: for thou hast been my defence and refuge in the day of my trouble.
17. Unto thee, O my strength, will I sing: for God is my defence, and the God of my mercy. (vv. 5, 11–17)

David prays for himself in Psalm 69:16, "Hear me, O Lord; for thy lovingkindness is good: turn unto me according to the multitude of thy tender mercies." Then his prayer continues with a view to the wicked.

22. Let their table become a snare before them: and that which should have been for their welfare, let it become a trap.
23. Let their eyes be darkened, that they see not; and make their loins continually to shake.
24. Pour out thine indignation upon them, and let thy wrathful anger take hold of them.
25. Let their habitation be desolate; and let none dwell in their tents.
26. For they persecute him whom thou hast smitten; and they talk to the grief of those whom thou hast wounded.
27. Add iniquity unto their iniquity: and let them not come into thy righteousness.
28. Let them be blotted out of the book of the living, and not be written with the righteous. (vv. 22–28)

The theory of general goodness is entirely without support in this passage and wholly in conflict with it. God's wrath and anger are over the ungodly. His loving-kindness is particular and over the righteous alone, for his loving-kindness is good, and therefore it cannot have the ungodly as its object.

For this reason his mercy is only toward those who fear him:

"As the heaven is high above the earth, so great is his mercy toward them that fear him" (Ps. 103:11). Those he pities, even as a father pities his children (v. 13). Upon those who fear him, keep his covenant, and remember his commandments to do them, his mercy is from everlasting to everlasting (vv. 17–18).

Psalm 104 sings of the goodness of God over all creatures, as it is manifested in all the works of God's hands. That the ungodly are excluded from this mercy and goodness is evident from verse 35: "Let the sinners be consumed out of the earth, and let the wicked be no more. Bless thou the Lord, O my soul. Praise ye the Lord."

The author of Psalm 109 invokes the terrible wrath of God on the ungodly: "Let this be the reward of mine adversaries from the Lord, and of them that speak evil against my soul." In the midst of his prayer he also sings, "But do thou for me, O God the Lord, for thy name's sake: because thy mercy is good, deliver thou me… Help me, O Lord my God: O save me according to thy mercy: that they may know that this is thy hand; that thou, Lord, hast done it" (vv. 20–27). Only in that light can one understand Psalm 125:4–5:

4. Do good, O Lord, unto those that be good, and to them that are upright in their hearts.
5. As for such as turn aside unto their crooked ways, the Lord shall lead them forth with the workers of iniquity: but peace shall be upon Israel.

How otherwise can we understand Psalm 136, which repeatedly praises the mercy of God as a reason for the effusion of his wrath over the ungodly and enemies of his cause? "To him that smote Egypt in their firstborn: for his mercy endureth forever"; and "overthrew Pharaoh and his host in the Red Sea: for his mercy endureth forever" (vv. 10, 15). Let Zwier explain how the one and same mercy gave Pharaoh all his power and glory, a mighty host, horses, and chariots and then caused him to perish with his host in the Red Sea.

17. To him which smote great kings: for his mercy endureth forever.
18. And slew famous kings: for his mercy endureth forever:
19. Sihon, king of the Amorites: for his mercy endureth forever:
20. And Og, king of Bashon: for his mercy endureth forever." (vv. 17–20)

The same thought is expressed as a prayer in Psalm 143:12: "Of thy mercy cut off mine enemies, and destroy all them that afflict my soul: for I am thy servant."

Always we meet with the same basic note in the psalms, and never do we find in them even a suggestion of a goodness and mercy of God toward the ungodly. Even Zwier knows that there is no support for his theory in the psalms, although he writes that often they sing of the general goodness of God. For "though the Lord be high, yet hath he respect unto the lowly: but the proud he knoweth afar off" (Ps. 138:6).

God executes judgment for the oppressed, gives food to the hungry, loosens the prisoners, opens the eyes of the blind, raises the bowed down, preserves the strangers, and relieves the fatherless and widows. But all his mercy and goodness are only for the righteous and do not concern the wicked at all. For, the Lord loves the righteous, but the way of the wicked he turns upside down (Ps. 146:7–9). The Lord lifts up the meek, but he casts the wicked down to the ground (Ps. 147:6).

These quotations from the psalms ought to make it very evident to Zwier that he has no right to accuse us of imposing our notions on the scriptures and of letting wretched human logic determine what its teachings must be.

It has become plain that the scriptures do not separate temporal things from eternal things. The mercy of God that is from eternity to eternity on those who fear him is upon them in time as well. The wrath of God that is from eternity to eternity on the reprobate ungodly abides on them in time as well. Scripture certainly does not induce or encourage superficiality. It never considers only what is visible and temporal and divorces it from the invisible and eternal. When Zwier desperately attempts to prove that his conception and that of the Christian Reformed Church harmonizes with what was published on this subject by some of the leading Reformed theologians in the Netherlands, he writes,

> Every Reformed man will agree with Greydanus when he declares that we can hardly speak of grace in the things that God gives to the nonelect upon earth, when we consider the eternal results caused by the abuse of those good gifts of God, so that it would have been better for the recipients of those gifts if they had never been born, and when we further consider what scripture teaches concerning the unchangeable counsel of God in which the terrible ultimate result was determined from eternity.
>
> When we speak of general or common grace, it is true that we remain on the surface of things and consider only what is visible and temporal. We do not penetrate in that case to the ground of things. But this is permissible because scripture gives us the example. (God's General Goodness, 26)

Every Reformed man agrees with what Greydanus wrote, but Zwier does not and his church does not. The first point of 1924 directly conflicts with Greydanus. Never did Zwier or any of the leaders of the Christian Reformed Church, who are so fond of the theory of common grace, concede that in the deepest sense common grace is really no grace at all. That church has unconditionally declared that there is in God a certain gracious disposition or attitude toward the ungodly reprobate.

The Current Teaching of Scripture (2)

Zwier must not practice accommodation when it appears that Reformed leaders such as Greydanus and Schilder do not agree with the view of common grace adopted by the Christian Reformed Church in 1924. In that case he faces two alternatives: he must admit that his church erred in 1924, or he must maintain that the above-mentioned theologians err.

But it certainly is not true that scripture induces us to be satisfied with remaining on the surface of things and thus to speak of common grace.

Chapter 8

The Current Teaching of Scripture (3)

The more one critically studies the doctrine of common grace—or general goodness or whatever name is given to this theory—in the light of scripture and the Reformed confessions, the more he becomes convinced that it is nothing but the Arminian view of grace applied to God's attitude to the reprobate wicked in this life.

It ought to be self-evident that one sails in Arminian waters when he teaches that God lavishes temporal blessings on the ungodly and that he intends to bless them in his loving-kindness when he gives them all the things of the present time, but that the ungodly turn these blessings into a curse on themselves. What else is this than the Arminian doctrine of free will and resistible grace applied to earthly and temporal things?

We all know that it is pure Arminianism to say that God intends to save the sinner and in his grace he offers salvation to him with the purpose of saving him, but that the sinner frustrates these good intentions of God and turns them into a curse. I say that we all know this, but even that did not appear to have been very clear in the consciousness of the synod of 1924, for in the first point the synod adopted the error that the preaching of the gospel is grace to all the hearers. Nevertheless, one who has any "Reformed feelings," as the president of that synod expressed it, immediately recognizes the Arminian error. Grace is not in the preaching *per se*, but in the divine operation of grace through the preaching, in the irresistible calling unto salvation. Even with respect to those who hear the gospel God is merciful to whom he will be merciful and whom he will he hardens.

Why should it be different with respect to temporal and earthly things, the things men have in common in this world? It ought not to be difficult to understand that rain and sunshine, gifts and talents, name and position, wealth and prosperity, floods and droughts, sickness and suffering, reproach and shame, and poverty and adversity are in themselves neither grace nor wrath, neither a blessing nor a curse, but that whether they serve as a blessing or as a curse depends on God's purposes with them and his works through them. God may curse through prosperity, and he may bless through adversity. Yet this is exactly what the defenders of common grace refuse to accept. They propose the strange doctrine that God is graciously disposed in time toward those on whom his wrath abides forever. He blesses in time those whom he eternally curses. This is maintained on the ground of the clearly Arminian principle that God intends to bless them, but they turn his blessing into a curse. God's gracious purposes are frustrated.

This presentation conflicts with the current teaching of scripture, for our God is in the heavens, and he has done whatsoever has pleased him. His intentions are never frustrated by the creature. Because Zwier said that the psalms are full of expressions referring to the general goodness of God, I quoted from them and found that they teach throughout that also in the things of the present time God's wrath abides on the ungodly. This will become clearer from other parts of the word of God.

Even a cursory reading of the book of Proverbs shows that it is strongly antithetical. Throughout it speaks of the sharp contrast between the godly and the ungodly, the righteous and the wicked, the wise and the foolish, those who love instruction and those who despise it, those who are of an understanding heart and the mockers, and of the twofold attitude and disposition of the Lord regarding them. Although the eternal destiny of both the righteous and the wicked is certainly taken into consideration in this book of Holy Writ, yet it deals chiefly with the manifestations of the righteous and the unrighteous and God's attitudes toward both in this life.

32. For the froward is abomination to the LORD: but his secret is with the righteous.
33. The curse of the LORD is in the house of the wicked: but he blesseth the habitation of the just.
34. Surely he scorneth the scorners: but he giveth grace unto the lowly.
35. The wise shall inherit glory: but shame shall be the promotion of fools. (Prov. 3:32–35)

It is plain from this passage that the words "froward," "wicked," "scorner," and "fool" refer to the same person. Wisdom is rooted in the fear of the Lord and is never found in the ungodly. Thus the words "righteous," "just," "lowly," and "wise" denote the same person. Thus there is a sharp contrast in these verses between the righteous and the wicked.

It is also clear that the passage speaks of God's attitude toward the righteous and the wicked in this life, in relation to and in connection with temporal things. The text speaks of the house of the wicked and the habitation of the just. There is no reference here to what Zwier calls saving grace. The text does not refer to what God will do with the righteous and the wicked after this life, in their eternal states, but pictures his attitude and disposition toward them in this world.

The passage leaves no room for the theory of a gracious disposition of God toward the ungodly in this present life. The text not only fails to speak of such a gracious attitude, but also definitely

The Current Teaching of Scripture (3)

denies and excludes it. No other interpretation of the text is possible. It speaks of God's *disposition* toward both the froward and the righteous: the froward is an abomination to him, while with the righteous is "his secret," which refers to the intimate fellowship of the covenant of his friendship, his grace. The contrast is very sharp. God's friendship and favor are with the righteous; God receives the righteous into his secret fellowship and causes him to taste his grace, but God will have nothing to do with the froward, who is an abomination to him and fills him with disgust. The operation of this twofold disposition is revealed in this life, in the dwellings of the righteous and the wicked. They each have a house. The dwelling of the wicked is even richer and more beautiful than that of the righteous, as the different terms "house" and "habitation," suggest and as is also the underlying supposition in verse 31, in which the righteous is exhorted not to envy the wicked. But however rich and convenient the house of the wicked may be, the curse of the Lord is there. Even through his temporal possessions God curses the ungodly. But the Lord blesses the habitation of the just. Be his house ever so humble and poor, the Lord blesses the righteous in that house and through the means of it.

Zwier alleges that he believes all this, but insists at the same time that God's goodness and loving-kindness are also over the ungodly and his blessing is in the house of the wicked. But we maintain that no man can actually believe these contradictions. One must choose. Either he must discard the theory of common grace, or general goodness, in the light of the clear teaching of the Bible, or he must deliberately reject and contradict this passage of Holy Writ. If there is a third possibility we will be glad to have Zwier show us.

Note the contrast in Proverbs 3:34–35. The scorners are the same as the wicked and the froward. The attitude and disposition of Jehovah are not only clearly described in the words, "surely he scorneth the scorners," but also can be deduced from the contrast, "he giveth grace unto the lowly." If these words do not mean that God gives no grace to the wicked, what do they mean? He laughs at them and puts them to shame and scorn. This also agrees with verse 35: "The wise shall inherit glory: but shame is the promotion of fools." This is the fruit of their own work. They heap shame on their heads. This is not to be understood as if the Lord had different intentions, as if he purposed to bless them and they turn his blessing into a curse and his glory into shame. On the contrary, entirely in harmony with God's attitude toward them and purpose concerning them, they carry their own shame. They are an abomination to the Lord; he scorns them; he curses them even through their houses, and he puts them to shame. As rational and moral creatures they work out their own shame in harmony with God's purpose and in the way of their wickedness.

Note also the antithesis in Proverbs 10: "Treasures of wickedness profit nothing: but righteousness delivereth from death. The Lord will not suffer the soul of the righteous to famish: but he casteth away the substance of the wicked" (vv. 2–3). "Blessings are upon the head of the just: but violence covereth the mouth of the wicked. The memory of the just is blessed: but the name of the wicked shall rot. The wise in heart will receive commandments: but a prating fool shall fall" (vv. 6–8). "The labour of the righteous tendeth to life: the fruit of the wicked to sin" (v. 16). "The fear of the wicked, it shall come upon him: but the desire of the righteous shall be granted" (v. 24). "The way of the Lord is strength to the upright: but destruction shall be to the workers of iniquity" (v. 29).

Where is the blessing of the Lord in those treasures of wickedness that profit nothing? Where is the loving-kindness of Jehovah in the substance of the ungodly, which he casts away, or in the violence that covers his mouth, or in his name that rots, or in the fruit of his labor, which is sin, or in the fear that comes on him, or in the destruction for him in the way of the Lord? It cannot be found. It is not. It is only with the righteous who is delivered from death,

The Current Teaching of Scripture (3)

whose soul God will not suffer to famish, upon whose head are blessings, whose memory is blessed, whose desire is granted, and for whom the way of the Lord is strength.

The theory of common grace does not know what to do with this doctrine of scripture, must have nothing of it, ignores it, contradicts it, and would like to apply all these passages to God's ultimate attitude toward the righteous and the wicked in their eternal states, in order to make room for a general goodness of God in this life. Yet, how clear it is that this is a distortion of the plain meaning of scripture!

Read the following verses from Proverbs: "They that are of a froward heart are abomination to the Lord: but such as are upright in their way are his delight" (11:20). "The wicked are overthrown, and are not: but the house of the righteous shall stand" (12:7). "There shall no evil happen to the just: but the wicked shall be filled with mischief. Lying lips are abomination to the Lord: but they that deal truly are his delight" (vv. 21–22). "The light of the righteous rejoiceth: but the lamp of the wicked shall be put out" (13:9). "The house of the wicked shall be overthrown: but the tabernacle of the upright will flourish" (14:11). "The wicked is driven away in his wickedness: but the righteous hath hope in his death" (v. 32). "In the house of the righteous is much treasure: but in the revenues of the wicked is trouble…The sacrifice of the wicked is an abomination to the Lord, but the prayer of the upright is his delight. The way of the wicked is an abomination to the Lord: but he loveth him that followeth after righteousness" (15:6–9). "The Lord will destroy the house of the proud: but he will establish the border of the widow. The thoughts of the wicked are an abomination to the Lord: but the words of the pure are pleasant words. The Lord is far from the wicked: but he heareth the prayer of the righteous" (vv. 25–26, 29). "The righteous man wisely considereth the house of the wicked, but God overthroweth the wicked for their wickedness" (21:12).

15. Lay not wait, O wicked man, against the dwelling of the righteous; spoil not his resting place:
16. For a just man falleth seven times and rises again: but the wicked shall fall into mischief.
17. Rejoice not when thine enemy falleth, and let not thine heart be glad when he stumbleth:
18. Lest the LORD see it, and it displease him, and he turn away his wrath from him.
19. Fret not thyself because of evil men, neither be envious at the wicked;
20. For there shall be no reward to the evil man; the candle of the wicked shall be put out. (24:15–20)

Let Zwier interpret these passages and harmonize them with his view of the general goodness of God. Let him not allege that he believes all this and seeks refuge in contradictions and absurdities. Without any reason or ground, and surely without an attempt to prove this, he complains that we have never yet explained the few texts to which he appeals in support of his theory of common grace, although we have repeatedly explained every one of them. But he surely never attempted and never will attempt to explain the above texts in the light of his theory of general goodness.

The same basic note is struck everywhere by the prophets of the Old Testament. Zwier imagines that he can show that the prophetic books of scripture teach a gracious disposition of God toward carnal and wicked Israel. However, he does not proceed to prove this.

Whoever is at all acquainted with the content of these books knows that the opposite is true. Moses' predictions concerning the blessing and the curse on the house of Israel are everywhere repeated and maintained by the prophets. The blessing of the Lord is on Israel that fears the Lord, trusts in him, and hopes in his promises. On that Israel is God's goodness, mercy, grace, and

The Current Teaching of Scripture (3)

loving-kindness. For Israel are his promises and his people will not be ashamed. But the wrath of God abides on carnal Israel, and his curse always strikes the ungodly.

We find this in the prophecy of Isaiah. The prophet's specific calling was to proclaim God's eternal mercy to the remnant according to the election of grace and his judgment to the hardened reprobate carnal element of the people. This hardening of the reprobate is accomplished through the same preaching whereby the elect are saved.

> 9. And he said, Go, and tell this people, Hear ye indeed, but understand not; and see ye indeed, but perceive not.
> 10. Make the heart of this people fat, and make their ears heavy, and shut their eyes; lest they see with their eyes, and hear with their ears, and understand with their heart, and convert, and be healed.
> 11. Then said I, Lord, how long? And he answered, Until the cities be wasted without inhabitant, and the houses without man, and the land be utterly desolate,
> 12. And the Lord have removed men far away, and there be a great forsaking in the midst of the land.
> 13. But yet in it shall be a tenth, and it shall return, and shall be eaten: as a teil tree, and as an oak, whose substance is in them, when they cast their leaves: so the holy seed shall be the substance thereof. (Isa. 6:9–13)

In Isaiah 57:19–21 we read,

> 19. I create the fruit of the lips; Peace, peace to him that is far off, and to him that is near, saith the Lord; and I will heal him.
> 20. But the wicked are like the troubled sea, when it cannot rest, whose waters cast up mire and dirt.
> 21. There is no peace, saith my God, to the wicked.

God's Goodness Always Particular

The same note is sounded by the other prophets.

5. I did know thee in the wilderness, in the land of great drought.
6. According to their pasture, so were they filled; they were filled, and their heart was exalted; therefore have they forgotten me.
7. Therefore I will be unto them as a lion: as a leopard by the way will I observe them:
8. I will meet them as a bear that is bereaved of her whelps, and will rend the caul of their heart, and there will I devour them like a lion: the wild beast shall tear them.
9. O Israel, thou hast destroyed thyself; but in me is thine help.
10. I will be thy king; where is any other that may save thee in all thy cities? and thy judges of whom thou saidst, Give me a king and princes?
11. I gave thee a king in mine anger, and took him away in my wrath.
12. The iniquity of Ephraim is bound up; his sin is hid.
13. The sorrows of a travailing woman shall come upon him: he is an unwise son; for he should not stay long in the place of the breaking forth of children. (Hosea 13:5–13)

The sacrifice and the prayer of the wicked are an abomination to the Lord; he turns a deaf ear to his hymns of praise. God's grace is over the righteous only.

21. I hate, I despise your feast days, and I will not smell in your solemn assemblies.
22. Though ye offer me burnt offerings and your meat offerings, I will not accept them: neither will I regard the peace offerings of your fat beasts.

The Current Teaching of Scripture (3)

23. Take thou away from me the noise of thy songs; for I will not hear the melody of thy viols.
24. But let judgment run down as waters, and righteousness as a mighty stream. (Amos 5:21–24)

God's attitude of wrath and vengeance to the wicked is expressed in Amos 9:1–4:

1. I saw the Lord standing upon the altar: and he said, Smite the lintel of the door, that the posts may shake: and cut them in the head, all of them; and I will slay the last of them with the sword: he that fleeth of them shall not flee away, and he that escapeth of them shall not be delivered.
2. Though they dig into hell, thence shall mine hand take them; though they climb up to heaven, thence will I bring them down:
3. And though they hide themselves in the top of Carmel, I will search and take them out thence; and though they be hid from my sight in the bottom of the sea, thence will I command the serpent, and he shall bite them:
4. And though they go into captivity before their enemies, thence will I command the sword, and it shall slay them: and I will set mine eyes upon them for evil, and not for good.

These last verses from Amos speak of men who are the objects of God's hot anger, whom the curse of the Lord pursues everywhere, so they cannot hide or escape from its destruction. There is certainly no room here for the loving-kindness of the Lord. Zwier will have to grant that there must be many exceptions to the general goodness of God and that it is not as general as he presents it. Common grace is not always and everywhere effective. All this is presented as taking place not in eternity but in time, not in hell but on the earth.

The same note is struck in Micah 6:9–16:

9. The Lord's voice crieth unto the city, and the man of wisdom shall see thy name: hear ye the rod, and who hath appointed it.
10. Are there yet the treasures of wickedness in the house of the wicked, and the scant measure that is abominable?
11. Shall I count them pure with the wicked balances, and with the bag of deceitful weights?
12. For the rich men thereof are full of violence, and the inhabitants thereof have spoken lies, and their tongue is deceitful in their mouth.
13. Therefore also will I make thee sick in smiting thee, in making thee desolate because of thy sins.
14. Thou shalt eat, but not be satisfied; and thy casting down shall be in the midst of thee; and thou shalt take hold but shalt not deliver; and that which thou deliverest I will give up to the sword.
15. Thou shalt sow, but thou shalt not reap; thou shalt tread the olives, but thou shalt not anoint thee with oil; and sweet wine, but thou shalt not drink wine.
16. For the statutes of Omri are kept, and all the works of the house of Ahab, and ye walk in their counsels; that I should make thee a desolation, and the inhabitants thereof an hissing; therefore ye shall bear the reproach of my people.

The ungodly in these verses are exceptions to Zwier's rule of God's general goodness. He takes the matter rather easy and quotes three texts in support of his view, speaking of them as a "threefold cord that cannot quickly be broken." On these verses he attempts to build an entire system of general doctrine that comprehends all men at all times and in all circumstances under a general grace of God. But he will have to admit that this general theory must fall. The word of God may occasionally speak in general terms when it contrasts the righteous and the wicked. But wherever it has the antithesis in view it certainly condemns the theory of common grace.

The Current Teaching of Scripture (3)

This is also evident from Nahum 1:2–7:

2. God is jealous, and the Lord revengeth; the Lord revengeth, and is furious; the Lord will take vengeance on his adversaries, and he reserveth wrath for his enemies.
3. The Lord is slow to anger, and great in power, and will not at all acquit the wicked: the Lord hath his way in the whirlwind and in the storm, and the clouds are the dust of his feet.
4. He rebuketh the sea, and maketh it dry, and drieth up all the rivers: Bashan languisheth, and Carmel, and the flower of Lebanon languisheth.
5. The mountains quake at him, and the hills melt, and the earth is burned at his presence, yea, the world and all that dwell therein.
6. Who can stand before his indignation? and who can abide in the fierceness of his anger? his fury is poured out like fire, and the rocks are thrown down by him.
7. The Lord is good, a strong hold in the day of trouble; and he knoweth them that trust in him.

God's goodness is particular. It is for those who trust in him, but he is furiously angry with the wicked.

Thus the prophets, as well as the psalmists, *want* it. For God's name's sake and his people's sake they must have nothing of the theory of a goodness and grace of God toward the wicked. Thus they confess, "Thou art of purer eyes than to behold evil, and canst not look on iniquity: wherefore lookest thou upon them that deal treacherously, and holdest thy tongue when the wicked devoureth the man that is more righteous than he?" (Hab. 1:13).

Well-known is the word of God in Malachi 1:2–4:

2. I have loved you, saith the Lord. Yet ye say, Wherein hast thou loved us? Was not Esau Jacob's brother? saith the Lord: yet I loved Jacob.

3. And I hated Esau, and laid his mountains and his heritage waste for the dragons of the wilderness.
4. Whereas Edom saith, We are impoverished, but we will return and build the desolate places; thus saith the Lord of hosts, They shall build, but I will throw down; and they shall call them, The border of wickedness, and, The people against whom the Lord hath indignation for ever.

Do not say that all this refers to eternity and that the wrath and hatred of God against Edom is compatible with the theory of God's general goodness in time. Although we readily admit that the text refers to God's eternal good pleasure, as is evident from the quotation of it in Romans 9:13, yet this eternal counsel of reprobation is presented in Malachi as manifesting itself in God's anger and curse against Esau in time. The theory of God's general goodness certainly does not apply to Edom, the type of the reprobate ungodly.

Nor does this theory of a general goodness of God find favor in the eyes of the Lord. It wearies him: "Ye have wearied the Lord with your words. Yet ye say, Wherein have we wearied him? When ye say, Every one that doeth evil is good in the sight of the Lord, and he delighteth in them; or, Where is the God of judgment?" (Mal. 2:17).

I have referred to such a large a number of passages from scripture to remove a false impression that Zwier has desperately attempted to make with his readers. It is the impression that our conviction that God's grace and goodness are always particular, only on his people, is without scriptural basis. Repeatedly he accuses us of philosophizing, of working with our wretched human logic rather than with the word of God. Besides, he left the impression that we have only a text or two that we make our hobby, and which he also readily accepts, although they are directly in conflict with his theory.

This wrong impression I would like to remove.

Chapter 9

The Current Teaching of Scripture (4)

In the New Testament Romans 1 first draws our attention regarding God's attitude or disposition toward an ungodly world outside of Christ. Especially verses 18–32 are of great importance because they speak of God's attitude toward the same heathen world that is also mentioned in Acts 14:16–17. This passage teaches that in times past God suffered all the heathen nations to walk in their own ways. Romans 1 repeatedly says that God gave over these same nations. Yet, according to Acts, God did not leave himself without witness in that heathen world. God's invisible things, even his eternal power and Godhead, are clearly seen from the creation of the world and are understood from the things that are made (Rom. 1:20). God did good from heaven, giving rain and fruitful seasons and filling the hearts with food and gladness (Acts 1:17). Nevertheless God's wrath was revealed from heaven over all ungodliness and unrighteousness of men who hold the truth in unrighteousness (Rom. 1:18).

It is striking that Abraham Kuyper Sr. refers to Romans 1 as one of the classic passages in support of his doctrine of common grace. One who reads that chapter without presuppositions must find this rather strange and surprising, for verses 18–32 speak of God's terrible wrath. God is not only terribly displeased with all iniquity, but also manifests his wrath, revealing it from heaven in history. These verses point to the ground and reason for God's wrath and its revelation from heaven: ungodly men who knew God but refused to glorify him and be thankful. And these verses vividly describe the awful operation of this wrath of God and its effect on the ungodly world, the misery and demoralization of the wicked. Of nothing but the wrath of God we read. How then can Kuyper discover in these verses a classic proof for the theory of common grace?

The answer is that Kuyper's conclusions are based on a distortion of the meaning of the passage rather than on a sound interpretation of it.

> However, this [that the wrath of God abides on the world] raises the question whether the world of mankind, that always revealed itself thus and was never any different throughout the ages and in all parts of the world, sank into this wretched condition willingly and knowingly or in spite of itself. Just suppose that the corruption of man's religious, moral, and intellectual life had worked through to the very end immediately after the fall, so that he would at once have sunk into the depths of complete destruction, then there would have been nothing to surprise us in this bestial and devilish condition of the world. This world would have become *hell itself* that very moment. It stands to reason that in such a hellish state the world could never reveal anything else than death, corruption, and iniquity. Who expects that the tiger will not kill, that the wolf will not take the prey, that the hawk will not prey on the dove? (Abraham Kuyper, *De Gemeene Gratie* [Common grace], 1:407; all translations from *De Gemeene Gratie* are mine.)

Kuyper's reasoning here has nothing to do with Romans 1, although he pretends to interpret it. He raises a question that is

The Current Teaching of Scripture (4)

not at all suggested by the text. What would have become of man and the world if death and corruption had reached its culmination immediately after the fall? Kuyper answers the question thus: the world would have turned into a hell with nothing but death, corruption, and iniquity. By this reasoning Kuyper intends to make room for the theory of a sin-restraining grace, for which there is no room in the text at all.

Kuyper's reasoning is based on the supposition that sin and death could have reached their culmination and worked through to the bitter end immediately after the fall. Then we would have had no world at all, but hell with two people. However, Romans 1 knows nothing of such a possibility.

On the basis of this supposition, Kuyper carries into the text the thought that somehow the development of corruption and death was not as fast as possible, for the operation of death and corruption was restrained. The syllogism is clear: If the working of death and corruption had not been restrained, the world would have become a hell immediately after the fall. It is clear that the present world is no hell. Hence the operations of death and corruption must have been checked. But the supposition of the major premise is false. This world could not have become a hell immediately after the fall. Hence the entire reasoning is false. Romans 1:18–32 teaches exactly the opposite, namely, that sin and corruption developed through history as fast as possible under the influence of the wrath of God revealed from heaven.

Thus Kuyper makes Romans 1 teach that the world is better than expected. The tiger does not kill, the wolf does not devour, and the hawk does not prey upon the dove. But Romans teaches exactly the opposite: the tiger kills, the wolf devours, and the hawk preys upon the dove; that is, the sinner commits all possible iniquities and proceeds from bad to worse as far as possible. If you carefully read the whole passage, you will find that it strongly emphasizes the actual corruption and iniquity of man.

Thus Kuyper makes room in the text for his theory of common grace. The text teaches that the world is hopelessly corrupt and wretched in sin and iniquity; Kuyper makes the text say that the world is better than expected.

He finds the thought that the natural man is not all darkness and iniquity. He writes, "With a view to this [that the world is better than expected], the apostle tells us that the condition of fallen man is absolutely not thus [utterly corrupt]. This is most strongly expressed in the words 'who knowing the judgment of God'" (Kuyper, *De Gemeene Gratie*, 1:407).

He means to say that the natural man's knowledge of the judgment of God proves that he is not in utter darkness. If sin had corrupted and darkened man's mind entirely, he would not have known the judgment or justice of God. But Kuyper only partly quotes verse 32. Only by doing this can he leave the impression that the fallen man is better than expected, that he is not all darkness, and that therefore there must be a restraining operation of common grace on him. However, when we read the whole of verse 32, we notice that the text teaches and emphatically intends to teach the exact opposite of what Kuyper makes of it—not that the natural man is better than expected, but that he is utterly bad and corrupt. The verse does not intend to teach that fallen man is still good enough to know the judgment of God, but it emphatically states that man is so bad that although he knows that judgment, he commits all iniquity and even takes pleasure in those who commit the same: "Who knowing the judgment of God, that they which commit such things are worthy of death, not only do the same, but have pleasure in them that do them" (v. 32).

Romans 1:18–23 presents the first stage of man's religious and moral degradation. It is the great abomination that fallen man changes the glory of the incorruptible God into the likeness of a creature, worships the brute beast, and bows before creeping things. However, Kuyper regards the practice of idolatry in the heathen world as a proof of common grace.

The Current Teaching of Scripture (4)

Especially this fact [that man changes the glory of the incorruptible God into the likeness of a creature and bows before it] is of primary importance for a right understanding of common grace.

Two things must be sharply discerned. First, idolatry itself proves the existence of common grace after the fall, for all idolatry evinces a need to worship. An animal does not worship God but neither does it practice idolatry. It lives and exists wholly without an idea or impulse of religion. And the damned in hell do not worship the Eternal One; neither do they commit idolatry. The devils indeed know the desire *to be* worshiped, but they cannot worship themselves. Suppose, then, that the development of sin had brought the human race immediately after the fall to the depth of spiritual and moral degradation, to a state of bestiality and utter confusion, then idolatry could not have originated. Therefore, the fact that idolatry arose wherever men lived is proof that the impulse to worship was preserved in man. That could not have been the case if common grace had not restrained the process of the utter degradation of man. (Kuyper, *De Gemeene Gratie*, 1:408–9)

This entire reasoning is based on the following false assumptions: the absence of idolatry among the devils is because sin is not restrained in them, there is no consciousness of God in devils and in ungodly man, in hell there will be no acknowledgment of God as God, and man apart from the restraining operation of common grace would have turned into an animal or a devil. I let that pass, but point out that by a meandering reasoning Kuyper makes Romans 1:18–32 teach exactly the opposite of what it actually teaches. Kuyper teaches that idolatry is proof of common grace. The text, however, points to idolatry as a manifestation of religious foolishness and degradation, a proof of the operation of God's wrath from heaven, by which the wicked, who refuse to glorify and give thanks to God, are made so utterly foolish that they bow in worship before four-footed beasts and creeping things.

In this way Kuyper carries the idea of common grace into the text, which, as anyone can see, is foreign to the entire passage. Thus he also prepares his readers for the interpretation that the terms "gave...up" and "gave...over" (vv. 24, 26, 28) signify a withholding of common grace.

> Now this [that the nations developed from bad to worse] the apostle explains from the fact that it pleased God to cause his common grace to be withdrawn. After the deluge common grace was increased, but now it is withdrawn again, and this withdrawal of common grace is described by the apostle Paul when he writes that God "gave them over to a reprobate mind." (Kuyper, *De Gemeene Gratie*, 1:411)

To "give...over" does not mean the same as to withdraw grace. There is a positive element in the first expression that is eliminated in the second. But apart from this, Kuyper contradicts himself in his reasoning process. His explanation certainly does not fit the text in Romans 1, for according to Kuyper one of the clearest manifestations of common grace must be found in the heathen nations' certain knowledge of God and of the judgment of God. If this were true, we certainly would expect that after God gave them over to a reprobate mind—withdrew his common grace—those heathen nations would gradually have lost the knowledge of God and of his righteous judgments, until finally they would have become like the animals. But this conclusion does not fit the facts. Everyone knows that in the countries about which the apostle is writing, especially Greece and Rome, idols abounded even after God gave the people over to a reprobate mind. And according to Kuyper the practice of idolatry is proof of the operation of common grace. But the verse that speaks of the knowledge those heathen nations had of God and of his judgments occurs at the end of this chapter. After

The Current Teaching of Scripture (4)

God gave them over to a reprobate mind, while they were wallowing in the mire of iniquity that was the result of being given over, they knew the judgment of God that they who do such things are worthy of death. The argument therefore contradicts itself: that the heathen know the righteous judgment of God is due to common grace; common grace is withdrawn; yet the heathen know the righteous judgment of God. Now we can understand how Kuyper concludes that Romans 1 is one of the classic chapters in favor of common grace.

However, if we read Romans 1 without any preconceived theory of common grace, we find that it teaches the opposite from common grace. It speaks of the wrath of God revealed from heaven over the ungodly. Instead of a restraint of sin, this chapter teaches an operation of the wrath of God whereby the ungodly proceeds from bad to worse: he is given over. Instead of picturing a natural man that is better than expected, this passage pictures the sinner in darkest and even horrible colors.

Not only therefore do we fail to find support in this passage of the word of God for Zwier's theory of God's general goodness, but also there is no room for general goodness alongside the wrath of God of which Romans 1 speaks. It is excluded. This passage does not speak of a wrath of God that will be revealed after the judgment day, but it speaks of wrath in the present time that operates from heaven on mankind as it exists in the world. The ungodly has knowledge of God. God never leaves himself without witness. He reveals himself in all the works of his hands. The invisible things of God from the creation of the world are clearly seen, being understood by the things that are made, even his eternal power and Godhead. What is known of God is manifest in them, for God shows it to them. But knowledge is no virtue. Nowhere does the word of God teach that this knowledge of God is proof of a kind of grace, or goodness, of God toward the ungodly. One may sweetly prate about gifts that we forfeited, which God graciously bestows on the ungodly, but that reasoning certainly does not harmonize with the language of Romans 1. The knowledge of God that the ungodly has is not presented as a forfeited gift or as a blessing of grace but as his *obligation* to glorify and to thank God. If the sinner had become an animal without any knowledge of God's eternal power and Godhead, he could not be expected to glorify and to serve the living God. But this is not true. He stands before God as a rational and moral creature. He knew God, and when he knew God, he refused to serve and to glorify God. This makes the ungodly the proper object of God's fierce wrath. The ungodly does not consider this natural knowledge of God as a blessing. He would like to rid himself of it if he could. He says in his heart that there is no God.

This explains the revelation of wrath from heaven of which Romans 1 speaks. The very fact that man knew God and would not serve him as God makes him the original object of God's wrath. God is terribly displeased with man's original and actual sins and will punish them in time and in eternity. When man holds the truth in unrighteousness, God's wrath is revealed from heaven upon him. It is revealed in its terrible operation, and this operation of God's wrath is the curse. This curse pursues man and makes him wretched and foolish and he bends the knee in worship before man, beast, and creeping things. Idolatry is no proof of grace, but is the result of the operation of God's wrath revealed from heaven. Man, who pretends to be wise, is made foolish by God in his wrath, so foolish that instead of calling upon the living God he seeks his refuge with brute beasts and dumb idols.

This wrath of God operates to the bitter end. This is the teaching of Romans 1, which does not teach a restraining grace but an always-pursuing wrath. Always this wrath abides on the ungodly. Always it presses him more deeply into degradation. Always it makes him more foolish, more wretched, and more of a reprobate mind. This is the meaning of the repeated "God gave them up" and "God gave them over" that occur in this chapter. The words do

The Current Teaching of Scripture (4)

not express a merely negative notion; they do not mean the same as "let go." They denote an operation of God's wrath whereby the ungodly wander away into the death-ways of their ungodliness and corruption to the end. They changed the truth of God into the lie. They glorified the creature in preference to the Creator. Let then that awful lie become fully manifest as the lie! That is God's purpose. That is the reason he gives them over. He does this through the sinful lusts of their own hearts. God's wrath operates upon and into those lusts, cursing and corrupting. They reveal themselves in all kinds of debauchery. They practice uncleanness. Men burn in their lusts one toward another, and men with men work that which is unseemly. Women seek satisfaction of their carnal lusts in ways contrary to nature. The ungodly are filled with all unrighteousness, fornication, wickedness, covetousness, maliciousness, envy, deceit, debate, murder, and malignity. They reveal themselves as whisperers, backbiters, haters of God, despiteful, proud, boasters, inventors of evil things, disobedient to parents, without understanding, covenant-breakers, without natural affection, implacable, and unmerciful. This corruption, wretchedness, death, and misery are the result of God's righteous wrath revealed from heaven over those who hold under the truth in unrighteousness.

Who, when he reads this chapter, still has any desire to speak of a general goodness of God?

Nor do we ever find different language in the New Testament. It knows nothing of a goodness, favor, grace, loving-kindness, and blessing of God on the ungodly reprobate. He who believes on the Son has everlasting life; he who obeys not the Son will not see life, but the wrath of God abides on him (John 3:36). God is merciful to whom he will be merciful and whom he will he hardens (Rom. 9:18). The scripture says that God raised Pharaoh for the purpose of manifesting God's power and wrath in Pharaoh and to serve the proclamation of God's glorious name over the whole earth. Unto this purpose he endures with much long-suffering the vessels of wrath fitted unto destruction (Rom. 9:17, 22–23). The elect indeed obtained salvation, but the rest were hardened. God gave them a spirit of slumber, eyes that they should not see and ears that they should not hear. Their table became a snare unto them, a trap, a stumbling block, and a recompense (Rom. 11:7–9). Unto those who are without, all "things are done in parables: that seeing they may see, and not perceive; and hearing they may hear, and not understand; lest at any time they should be converted, and their sins should be forgiven them (Mark 4:11–12). "Therefore they could not believe, because Esaias said again, He hath blinded their eyes, and hardened their heart; that they should not see with their eyes, nor understand with their heart, and be converted, and I should heal them" (John 12:39–40). God resists the proud, but he gives grace to the lowly (1 Pet. 5:5).

Zwier may deny all this and attempt to maintain his distinction between saving grace and nonsaving grace, but he cannot deny that all these verses speak of God's wrath operating in time, in this world, and in and through the things that the ungodly receive. In this world God is angry with the wicked, reveals his wrath, makes the ungodly miserable and foolish, hardens him, and through the things of the present time, even through prosperity, sets him on slippery places and casts him into destruction.

If only Zwier would acknowledge this, and if only he could pierce the mists of common grace that now bedim his understanding, he could maintain the current doctrine of Holy Writ and confess that God's goodness is not for the wicked but is always particular. And he could interpret the few texts he quotes as teaching common grace in the light of this current teaching of the Bible.

Chapter 10

Temporal Things in the Light of Eternity

I have sufficiently demonstrated that the word of God throughout teaches that God's goodness is always particular. The passages to which I referred allow no other interpretation. They speak of God's blessing on the righteous and his curse on the ungodly not as a truth that only pertains to eternity but also as a reality in the present time. Those passages leave no room for the distinction between a saving and a nonsaving goodness of God. In time and in eternity God is terribly displeased with the wicked, and they are the objects of his consuming wrath. It is now up to those who maintain that God in the present time is favorably disposed to the ungodly to interpret the numerous passages of Holy Writ to which I called attention and to make plain that my interpretation is erroneous. Unless they do this I take their silence as an admission that they know of no interpretation that befits their theory.

How must the temporal things, which the ungodly receive in common with the righteous, be explained? There is no dispute that in this world the righteous and the unrighteous have all temporal things in common. Our first parents did not go to hell immediately after the fall, and the world did not become chaotic. Adam and Eve did not return to the dust, but the human race continued to exist. Also the ungodly are born and live threescore and ten years, or if they are very strong, fourscore years. They too receive talents, gifts, and means. God rains on the righteous and the unrighteous, and the sun rises on both. They have houses, clothes, food, and drink. They enjoy the same relationships as the righteous in home and in society. They develop and find the means of their development in the earthly creation. All this is of God, who even frequently gives them more earthly and temporal gifts than the righteous receive.

If God's goodness is always and only over the righteous, how must it be explained that the ungodly also receive all these things and God fills their hearts with food and gladness?

From this fact many conclude that God in this life is gracious to the ungodly and favorably disposed to the wicked. The argument is plain and appears reasonable. The temporal things the ungodly receive are good things. They enjoy them. If God gives good things to the ungodly, is not this sufficient proof of his goodness and favor toward them? If you object to the term *common grace* because you would rather use the term *grace* exclusively with reference to salvation or to employ some other word such as *goodness,* do not deny the fact: earthly and temporal things are *blessings* of God, and God's blessings manifest his goodness and favor. It surely cannot be maintained that God blesses in his wrath. Therefore, common grace really needs no proof. It is utterly foolish to deny it because it is seen every day. Rain and sunshine are common grace.

By such reasoning from experience, not from scripture, people generally conclude that there is common grace. From what they observe in the world and from a superficial interpretation of what they perceive, they deduce the doctrine of common grace. After they have thus interpreted the facts of their experiences, they turn to scripture to corroborate their theory.

However, if we are not satisfied with scanning the surface of things, but desire to look more deeply into them, we soon understand that the first deduction is erroneous and that we cannot conclude that God is graciously disposed to anyone merely because he

Temporal Things in the Light of Eternity

receives temporal and material things. Hence we want to consider the significance of temporal things in the light of what we find to be the current teaching of scripture.

Besides, there are a few passages that the defenders of common grace quote that seem to teach God's favorable disposition to the wicked and to the righteous in this world. We must consider these passages to find their true meaning in agreement with the current teaching of the word of God.

This is the proper procedure. First, we ascertained what the Bible teaches throughout regarding God's attitude to the righteous and the wicked in this world. Then we turn to the few passages that appear to be in conflict with the general doctrine of scripture and interpret them according to the rule of scripture.

Zwier refuses to apply this method, which is the only proper method that Reformed theologians have always applied. He is afraid that this procedure is rationalistic. He insists that regarding this point there are two series of scriptural texts that cannot be harmonized. Zwier refuses to attempt to bring them into agreement with each other. He maintains and believes that God's goodness as manifest in temporal things is particular and general. He alleges to believe fully what is taught in Psalm 73 and Psalm 92, but he thinks that Matthew 5:45 and Acts 14:16–17 teach the opposite. Therefore, he finds a dilemma, and he wants to accept both horns of it.

I will, however, follow the Reformed procedure in interpreting scripture.

Zwier's reasoning that God is favorably disposed toward the wicked in this world because he sends them rain and sunshine and bestows on them temporal things is untenable. Even if we consider these temporal things by themselves, apart from their relation to and significance for eternity, they may not without reservation be called good. They are not unmixed. They are all limited by and lie within the scope of temporal death. Death is in them all. Even if we leave eternal things out of consideration and remain on the surface of temporal things, the fact is that with all things we all lie in the midst of death. This life is nothing but a continual death. Death works in our members and gnaws at the very roots of our existence from the moment we are born. We die every day. All things are corruptible. We eat and drink and breathe corruption. The shadow of death spreads over our temporal lives. The fear of death pursues us. Forget for a moment the difference between the righteous and the wicked. Look at the temporal things alone and do not consider them in the light of their eternal significance, and what you have left is nothing more than that men perish like the beasts. The conclusion of the preacher then must certainly be ours: "Vanity of vanities…all is vanity" (Eccl. 12:8). For anyone who does not close his eyes entirely to the vanity of life and the suffering and death of the present time, pessimism, with its slogan that life is not worth living, must seem to be the only true philosophy. If you view temporal things in this light, they all lie within the sphere and power of death, and they all inevitably end in death. God causes us to be born in order to kill us. Then there is really no grace at all. "By thy wrath we pine and die," we may well lament, for God's anger heavily presses on the whole of our temporal existences.

However, if you are not so pessimistically inclined, you can close your eyes, at least partly, to this grim reality. In that case you will try to withdraw certain things from this terrible wrath of God. You will make a distinction between good and evil things. The preacher looked through spectacles that were too darkly tinted. All is not vanity. There is still much good in life. The world is better than expected or than the pessimist would have us believe. Men can enjoy many things in this short span of life, and these good things are manifestations of God's grace.

Still death is your farthest horizon; still you do not view temporal things in the light of eternity. While God punishes us with death in his wrath, he still gives us many things to enjoy. This is his general grace, favor, goodness, or whatever term you prefer, of which both the righteous and the wicked are objects. Then you confront another problem. Turn where you will and death will meet you everywhere. If there are good things in life, the evil things are abounding. If there is joy and gladness in this world, it is the joy of the death cell, and the suffering of this present time abounds. Also this suffering is general and common. Not only the wicked, but also the righteous receive the evil things of life. If from the fact that the wicked receive good things in this life you conclude that God is favorably disposed to the wicked as well as to the righteous, you are also bound to conclude from the fact that evil things are common to the righteous and the wicked that God's wrath is upon them both. Then all things are common, and there is no difference between the righteous and the wicked in this world. God's attitude toward both is the same. Then in this present time nothing is particular. Grace and anger, loving-kindness and anger, love and hatred, and the blessing and the curse are all common.

To maintain the theory of common grace, it is not sufficient to be satisfied with looking on the surface of things. To believe this theory one must also refrain from explaining the things he beholds on that surface.

Let us inquire of scripture whether it is true that the things of this life are to be regarded as manifestations of God's gracious disposition toward the wicked. I repeatedly have called attention to the clear teachings of Psalm 73 and Psalm 92, not has if these two passages are the only texts that condemn common grace and teach that in this life God's grace is always particular, as Zwier seems to imply. But these two psalms shed a very clear light on how we must conceive of God's attitude and disposition toward the ungodly in view of their receiving from him all the things of this present life in common with the godly. Both psalms view the things of the present time in the light of eternity. This is evident from even a superficial reading. They consider all things in the light of God's eternal thoughts, his eternal counsel, and with a view to the eternal destiny of men.

In Psalm 73 we read first of Asaph's experience when he looked on the surface of things and thus attempted to understand God's providential government of men. He had no peace. His feet were almost gone, his steps had almost slipped. He confronted a problem. He contemplated the works of God. The poet was anxious and concerned not about earthly things, but about the glory of his God. When he considered temporal things, it appeared as if God was favorably disposed to the ungodly. They seemed to have peace. They prospered in the world. Their eyes stood out with fatness. They had more than their hearts could wish. There were no bands even in their death. Yet the poet was plagued the whole day and chastened every morning. In vain he had cleansed his heart and washed his hands in innocence. The attitude of the poet was radically different from the attitude of those who love to speak of God's grace to the wicked and expel from the fellowship of their churches those who insist that God loves the righteous and hates the workers of iniquity. That God would love the wicked Asaph could not believe; the very thought was offensive to him. Thus he was almost inclined to ask, "How does God know? Is there knowledge in the Most High?" Although he refrained from actually asking these questions, the matter was nevertheless too painful for him to understand.

All this changed when he went into the sanctuary of God. God led him into the sanctuary, caused him to descend from the surface into the depth of things, and made him see those same temporal things in their reality, in the light of God's eternal counsel and purpose. What did he see there? Did he then learn to accept the theory of common grace and find peace in it? On the contrary, he discovered he had erred when he thought he was justified in concluding that God was gracious to the wicked because they prosper in the world. He perceived that God's wrath is always against the wicked, that his curse is even in their houses, that his wrath is even in the things they receive in the present time, and that their present prosperity is a slippery road on which God leads them to eternal destruction. When you consider temporal things in the light of eternity, you must abandon the theory of common grace. Such is the clear teaching of Psalm 73.

Repeatedly Zwier assures his readers that he fully accepts the teaching of Psalm 73. Yet he would also maintain that God is graciously disposed to the wicked in the present time and that this favorable disposition is manifested in the temporal prosperity of the ungodly. But this is impossible. If Psalm 73 teaches that the temporal prosperity of the wicked is not a proof of God's grace to them, but plainly reveals that God intends and uses the things of the present time as means to bring the wicked to eternal destruction, and if one asserts that he wholeheartedly accepts this truth in all its implications, then he denies the theory of common grace. One cannot again ascend from the depth of God's sanctuary, where he has been instructed in God's holy purposes, to the surface of merely human contemplation, in which it appears to him that God is graciously disposed to the wicked and the righteous alike. One may be quite sure that Asaph, after he had seen temporal things in the true light of the sanctuary of God, would never agree with Zwier's theory of a general goodness, or grace, of God.

Psalm 92 is no less clear on this subject.

1. It is good to give thanks unto the LORD, and to sing praises unto thy name, O most High;
2. To shew forth thy lovingkindness in the morning, and thy faithfulness every night,
3. Upon an instrument of ten strings, and upon the psaltery; upon the harp with a solemn sound.
4. For thou, LORD, hast made me glad through thy work: I will triumph in the works of thy hands.
5. O LORD, how great are thy works! and thy thoughts are very deep.
6. A brutish man knoweth not; neither doth a fool understand this.

7. When the wicked spring as the grass, and when all the workers of iniquity do flourish; it is that they shall be destroyed forever" (vv. 1–7).

This song for the Sabbath is designed to be sung by the church for the special purpose of singing of God's loving-kindness. The psalm knows of no distinction between a saving and a nonsaving loving-kindness, or grace, of God. It simply speaks of *the* loving-kindness of God. But if one is to sing of the loving-kindness of the Most High, he must do it so that God's name is praised and magnified by the song. He must remember that God is the faithful one (v. 2) and that he is upright and there is no unrighteousness in him (v. 15). This faithfulness and uprightness belong to the holy name of God, and in a song to the praise of God's loving-kindness, his righteousness may not be forgotten or eliminated. One must sing intelligently of God's loving-kindness, meditating (with a "solemn sound") to the accompaniment of the harp. One must be Reformed even in his singing!

The psalmist learned to know God's loving-kindness and faithfulness and the greatness and glory of his name from the works of his hands. That the Lord shows loving-kindness and to whom he shows loving-kindness are evident from his works. But if one would truly know and understand these works of the Most High, he must not consider the surface of temporal and earthly things. But he must descend into the depths of God's thoughts and purposes, for the works of the Lord are very great and the thoughts of his heart are very deep. If you would rejoice in the works of the Lord and praise him for his glorious deeds, you must exert yourself to contemplate them seriously in the light of revelation.

These great works of the Lord and his very deep thoughts are especially manifested in the wicked and all the workers of iniquity, *in order that* they may be destroyed forever. Also in this psalm the subject is the temporal things that the ungodly receive from the

Temporal Things in the Light of Eternity

Lord. And they do receive many things. The wicked grow as the grass, and all the workers of iniquity flourish. They enjoy great prosperity. In this psalm temporal things are viewed and judged in the light of eternity. The psalm mentions God's deep thoughts and his eternal purposes with all things. These eternal purposes concern the eternal destiny of the wicked, their everlasting destruction, and their present prosperity as means to prepare them for their eternal destiny. The wicked grow and flourish in order to be destroyed forever. Such are the Lord's deep thoughts and eternal purposes.

In these works God must be known. And when the church on the Sabbath sings of God's loving-kindness, she may not leave these eternal purposes and divine thoughts out of consideration. Thus this psalm clearly teaches that God's goodness and loving-kindness are never general or common and that the wicked are never the objects of his grace. Emphatically the psalm warns against the conclusion that because the wicked prosper in this world God is favorably disposed toward them. It may appear so on the surface, but if in the light of revelation you know God's deep and eternal thoughts and purposes, you perceive that things are not what they seem to be.

Only when you have learned to see and acknowledge all this, can you sing of the loving-kindness of the Lord. When you consider the mere surface of things, you may be pricked in your reins as Asaph was; you may envy the ungodly; you may be inclined to say there is no knowledge in the Most High; and then you cannot sing at all. Or you may thoughtlessly and superficially sing of God's loving-kindness over the wicked, of a common and general goodness of the Most High, whereby his faithfulness and his righteousness are denied; but you cannot sing of the loving-kindness of the Lord, for it is never common. To do this you must enter into the sanctuary, descend into the depths of God's secrets and of his deep thoughts as revealed in his word, and in the light of them consider all temporal things.

The foolish and brutish man remains on the surface of things and refuses to consider them in the light of God's revelation. He superficially contemplates temporal things apart from their eternal significance and does not know and understand these things. He foolishly speaks of common grace or general goodness, of God's loving-kindness toward the wicked in this life, because he does not know the deep thoughts of God and does not understand his great works. Because he merely scans the surface of things, he cannot understand that God sends prosperity to the wicked in his fierce anger and to destroy them forever. He considers all the things of this life as many presents that God bestows on the ungodly in his loving-kindness for their pleasure and enjoyment.

Zwier assures us that he also believes what the word of God teaches in Psalm 92. He even admits that only the foolish and brutish man who is satisfied with the surface of things can speak of common grace. If only he would be consistent and adhere to this truth throughout his teaching!

Alas! While he assures us that he believes all this, he persistently denies it. He prefers to scan the surface of things.

Chapter 11

The Triple Cord: Psalm 145:9

We now confront the question whether or not it is possible to explain the scriptural passages that Zwier quotes in support of his view of a general goodness of God in harmony with the current teaching of the Bible that God's goodness is always particular. If we succeed in doing this, our position against those who teach common grace is strengthened.

If in some instances this would appear to be beyond our power, we will acknowledge that we do not fully understand those particular texts; but even then the current teaching of scripture must stand. We will refrain from raising an entire structure of doctrine on the foundation of a few individual passages, as Zwier attempts to do, especially if the dogma so construed conflicts with the general teaching of Holy Writ.

This method of interpreting a few passages of scripture in the light of the analogy of scripture is not the same as permitting one's exegesis of the Bible to be influenced and dominated by dogmatic preconceptions. Dogmatics may not determine the results of exegesis. Exegesis must be free. To bind the interpretation of scripture to preconceived dogmas is certainly un-Reformed, as it is un-Reformed to let synodical declarations determine one's explanation of certain texts. But it is certainly in harmony with the Reformed method of interpretation to explain the word of God in its own light. This method I will apply in opposition to Zwier's method. He insists that this may not be done, although his method results in contradictions and absurdities.

We begin our study with texts that were first discovered by the Kalamazoo synod of 1924 as teaching general, or common, grace and that Zwier adduces to prove the same theory. According to him they constitute a "threefold cord…[that] cannot easily be broken." These texts are Psalm 145:9, Acts 14:16–17, and Luke 6:35. According to Zwier these three passages are sufficient to establish the doctrine of common grace.

> The scriptural proof becomes gradually more stringent: God's goodness is spread over all men without distinction; over all the heathen who have no knowledge of the true God; yea, even over the ungodly who have some knowledge of him but set themselves in enmity against him.
>
> What riches of loving-kindness!
>
> These scriptural declarations constitute a threefold cord, which according to the wise king cannot easily be broken (Eccl. 4:12).
>
> The truth of Solomon's words was corroborated among us. How many attempts were made by the brethren who deny common grace to break that triple cord! But they never were and never will be successful. These texts speak too clearly for that. (God's General Goodness, 18)

We must call attention to Psalm 145:9: "The LORD is good to all: and his tender mercies are over all his works."

Earlier I offered an explanation of this text, but what Zwier says about this verse needs to be investigated in more detail. First he tries to overthrow our exegesis of the text. With boasting contempt he declares that our interpretation is so evidently corrupt that it is a mystery to him how anyone "with even a quarter of an ounce of exegetical brains could be convinced by it" (God's General Goodness, 15).

We would expect that one who judges so contemptuously the work of others would at least be thoroughly acquainted with it. We justly expected Zwier to be aware of our interpretation of this text, but we are disappointed. He knows literally nothing about our explanation of the passage. He evidently never acquainted himself with our exegesis. He condemns without knowing what he condemns. He seems to think that our interpretation of Psalm 145:9 is fairly presented in the following words:

> No one has the right to read something between the lines here, to add something to the text that is not expressed. This is what the brethren who deny common grace do. They want us to read in the text that the Lord gives good gifts to all men; or that the Lord is good to all the elect, and his mercies are over all his works in the realm of redemption. (God's General Goodness, 15)

Later Zwier elaborates on what he means.

> Sometimes they say that this statement must be understood in the sense that God gives good gifts to all men. God's gifts, even when they are bestowed on the ungodly, are always good. God never gives anything else than good gifts. But they allege that God bestows these good gifts on the wicked with the purpose to lead them to destruction. And thus we must also understand this text in harmony with that notion.
>
> But usually the opponents of common grace prefer a different interpretation of this text. They claim that in the light of the entire psalm we must understand that verse 9 refers to God's people only: the Lord is good to all the elect. (God's General Goodness, 15)

Then Zwier proceeds to show why neither of these two interpretations is acceptable.

It is deplorable that he never quotes our writings or even gives any references to passages of our writings to prove that we actually explain the texts as he claims we do. Probably it suited his purpose better to keep this secret and to take the liberty of informing his readers about our methods of scriptural interpretation in his own words. No doubt he was surer of successfully attaining the purpose of impressing his readers with the utter folly of our interpretation if he did not quote us literally or even place his readers in a position to check his allegations. But we are inclined to ask, in actual practice and life does Zwier believe in the accountability of man?

Difficult though this was, since Zwier gave no references to our writings, we checked his statements. Although it seemed extremely improbable that we ever offered the exegesis of Psalm 145:9 he ascribed to us, we perused again most of our writings on this subject. The result was as might be expected. Zwier is guilty of gross misrepresentation. Never did we offer as an interpretation of Psalm 145:9 that God gives good gifts to all men, nor did we suggest that the word *elect* must be inserted into the text. In one of our articles in the *Standard Bearer* we quoted one of the marginal notes in the Dutch *Statenbijbel*, which reads in English, "To wit, of such as are able to receive his mercies," which may prove that also our Dutch fathers must fall under Zwier's condemnation as having not a quarter of an ounce of exegetical sense. But never did we interpret the text as he alleges. He wholly misrepresents us. He has all the more reason to be ashamed because he was in a position to know better and he uses his misrepresentations as a pretext to heap contempt on our interpretations of scripture.

What is his exegesis of this passage? I quote:

> It stands to reason that one turns first to Psalm 145:9.
>
> This passage really needs no explanation. It is so clear that a child has no difficulty understanding it. "The Lord

is good to all." The meaning is that God's goodness is extended to all men.

That the word "all" in this text may not be understood in the limited sense, but must be applied to all men, follows necessarily from what immediately follows in the same verse: "and his tender mercies are over all his works."

Both expressions are as general as possible. God's goodness is spread over "all," and his tender mercies are over "all his works." The two declarations supplement each other. "All" is more definitely explained by "all his works."

You have no right to read something between the lines here or to add something that is not expressed.

At once we express our wholehearted agreement with the last statement. We may not add anything to the text that is not expressed, if we understand Zwier's last clause to imply "and that does not follow from the context."

Although Zwier apparently understands this rule well, he does not apply it, but entirely ignores it in his interpretation of the text and does exactly the opposite. He inserts something into the text that is not stated in the text or implied in the context. He adds the very important word *men*. Instead of reading the text as it stands, Zwier reads it as "the Lord is good to all *men*." This is not the text. The text is "the Lord is good to all."

The context does not give the right to insert the word *men* into the text. We wholly agree with Zwier that according to the rule of Hebrew parallelism, one half of this verse supplements and explains the other: "all" in the first clause is more definitely explained by "all his works" in the second clause. If this is evident, it must be applied. It is evident that "all his works" is not the same as all men. That Zwier seems to think they are the same shows that even men who weigh their exegetical ability by a quarter of an ounce sometimes make mistakes. If he had applied his own rule, he would not have read the first clause as "the Lord is good to all men." If anything had to be inserted into the first clause, it should have been taken from the second clause, so that the first clause would be "the Lord is good to all his works." Or if one would rather avoid the same word, the first clause could be rendered as "the Lord is good to all his creatures." Zwier's interpretation of the word "all" is too limited. He wants to limit it to men; whereas, the text refers to all creatures, to all the works of God.

That this is the true interpretation should have been plain to Zwier from the context in verses 15–16: "The eyes of all wait upon thee; and thou givest them their meat in due season. Thou openest thine hand, and satisfiest the desire of every living thing." This passage also contains "all": "the eyes of all wait upon thee." Also in this text "all" is explained by what follows: "and satisfiest the desire of every living thing. Here too the concept is broader than what is expressed by the word *men*; it also includes the animals.

Against this it cannot be objected that one cannot say of animals that their eyes wait upon the Lord and that therefore "all" must refer to men. To urge such an objection reveals ignorance with regard to scripture's usual way of speaking of the whole creation: the creature is included in God's covenant. Besides, in answer to this objection, we can point to Psalm 104:24–29:

> 24. O LORD, how manifold are thy works! in wisdom hast thou made them all: the earth is full of thy riches.
> 25. So is this great and wide sea, wherein are things creeping innumerable, both small and great beasts.
> 26. There go the ships: there is that leviathan, whom thou hast made to play therein.
> 27. These wait all upon thee; that thou mayest give them their meat in due season.
> 28. That thou givest them they gather: thou openest thine hand, they are filled with good.
> 29. Thou hidest thy face, they are troubled: thou takest away their breath, they die, and return to their dust.

The Triple Cord: Psalm 145:9

It is evident that Zwier's interpretation of Psalm 145:9 cannot be maintained. His insertion of the word *men* is not permissible. It is contrary to the clear meaning of the text, and it does not harmonize with the context of the psalm. It is difficult to understand how he could think this explanation is the proper one, unless he desired to support the exegesis suggested by the Kalamazoo synod. His opinion is that the text is so clear it needs no interpretation and a child can understand it. Yet he offers an explanation that anyone can readily see does not fit the text. Perhaps he relied too much on his opinion that the text is very simple and needs no explanation. Or he may have been somewhat predisposed to his interpretation by the desire to keep the text as a proof for his theory of God's general goodness. However, he will certainly have to admit his error and acknowledge that he had no right to insert the word *men* into the text.

He will also have to confess that he misrepresented us when he informed his readers about our alleged explanation of this text. We certainly do not and never did interpret the text as if it said that God gives good gifts to all men, nor do we intend to insert the word *elect* or anything similar. All that Zwier writes on this matter is entirely beside the point.

We read the text as follows: "The LORD is good to all his creatures, and his tender mercies are over all his works." We too insert something, and we do that wherever the word "all" occurs in the Bible without further limitation. The word "all" demands this, for without some modifying word "all" has no meaning. It requires a modifier because by itself it is indefinite. But only the text and the context may determine what the modifying word should be. We may not arbitrarily insert a word according to our notions or to suit our preconceived ideas and theories. Only the word of God may determine our choice of the limiting word. With respect to Psalm 145:9, it is not difficult to determine the word. What modifier should be added is so clear that it can only cause surprise that one could miss it. The text almost literally mentions the word. The whole verse in its context is most naturally read thus: "The Lord is good to all his creatures, and his tender mercies are over all his works."

Perhaps, you ask what is the difference between this interpretation and Zwier's? Do we not broaden the concept rather than limit it? He reads *all men;* we prefer *all creatures.* It would seem that the all men are included in all creatures. Therefore, this passage is a proof for a general goodness of God.

In a certain sense we do have a broader concept of God's goodness than those who teach the theory of common grace. But our difference with them is exactly that their general goodness of God is *common,* while ours is always *particular.* They insist that righteous and wicked are alike the objects of the general goodness of the Lord. God's favor, grace, mercy, and loving-kindness are common. Because of this they insert into Psalm 145:9 the word *men* rather than the self-evident *creatures.*

The word of God will have nothing of such a common, general goodness of the Most High that makes the wicked the objects of his love. True, scripture plainly teaches that God's goodness includes not only men, but also other creatures. The beasts of the field, the fowls of the air, the fish of the sea, the young ravens, the wild goats, the strong leviathans, the trees of the woods, the flowers of the field, the tender grass, the green herbs, the golden sun, the moon with her mellow light, the twinkling stars, the ever-restless sea, the majestic rivers, and the meandering brooks,—all these are the objects of God's goodness. His mercies are over all his works. All these creatures, according to God's covenant with Noah, are taken up into his covenant. Of this all-comprehensive nature of the covenant of God, the rainbow is displayed in the clouds as a sign.

Of this mercy of God over all his creatures many of the psalms sing, as does Psalm 104:10–24:

> 10. He sendeth the springs into the valleys, which run among the hills.

The Triple Cord: Psalm 145:9

11. They give drink to every beast of the field: the wild asses quench their thirst.
12. By them shall the fowls of the heaven have their habitation, which sing among the branches.
13. He watereth the hills from his chambers: the earth is satisfied with the fruit of thy works.
14. He causeth the grass to grow for the cattle, and herb for the service of man: that he may bring forth food out of the earth;
15. And wine that maketh glad the heart of man, and oil to make his face to shine, and bread which strengtheneth man's heart.
16. The trees of the LORD are full of sap; the cedars of Lebanon, which he hath planted;
17. Where the birds make their nests: as for the stork, the fir trees are her house.
18. The high hills are a refuge for the wild goats; and the rocks for the conies.
19. He appointed the moon for seasons: the sun knoweth his going down.
20. Thou makest darkness, and it is night: wherein all the beasts of the forest do creep forth.
21. The young lions roar after their prey, and seek their meat from God.
22. The sun ariseth, they gather themselves together, and lay them down in their dens.
23. Man goeth forth unto his work and to his labour until the evening.
24. O LORD, how manifold are thy works! in wisdom hast thou made them all: the earth is full of thy riches.

According to God's eternal covenant these creatures, which are now subject to vanity, will be liberated from the bondage of corruption to share in the glorious liberty of the children of God (Rom. 8:19–22).

If Zwier will sing of the loving-kindness and mercy of God over all his creatures, gladly will we join him. The word of God abundantly witnesses of this goodness of the Lord.

But we earnestly protest, in the name of that same holy scripture, against any attempt to make the loving-kindness of the Lord common and to let the church of Christ sing of a grace or favor of God over the righteous and wicked alike. This makes God common. God's goodness is over all his creatures, and the ungodly are right in the midst of the manifestations of God's goodness, but they have no part in them. They are not the objects of them. The wrath of God abides on them.

This is plain from Psalm 145:20: "The LORD preserveth all them that love him: but all the wicked will he destroy."

Zwier can find no proper place for this verse in his conception. He finds one of his anomalies, one of his contradictions there.

> We do not at all detract from the truth that the psalmist expresses in verse 20. The Lord certainly preserves all those who love him. The rest he does not preserve; he destroys all the ungodly. That we confess without any reservation. But this truth does not exclude in the least the other truth, professed in verse 9; namely, that there is also a nonsaving goodness of the Lord, in which all men in this life, also the ungodly, have a part. It is only temporal prosperity, no eternal gain, which through the general loving-kindness of God they receive; and it will serve to make their judgment severer in the day of days. Be it so. But this does not give anyone the right to deny that this also is really a goodness of God. You say that you cannot harmonize these two? We confess to the same incapability. (God's General Goodness, 15)

The Triple Cord: Psalm 145:9

However, the conflict of which Zwier speaks does not exist. That it does seem to exist before Zwier's consciousness is because he inserts into verse 9 the word *men*, while he should have added the word *creatures*. Replace the word *men* with *creatures*, and there is nothing left of the imaginary disharmony between verses 9 and 20. Surely the Lord is good to all his creatures, to man and beast and the green tree, but not to all men. The ungodly are the exception; they are the objects of God's wrath, and God surely will destroy them.

Thus there is no dilemma. Thus the text perfectly harmonizes with the current teaching of Holy Writ that God's goodness is always particular.

Thus one of the strands of Zwier's threefold cord is broken.

Chapter 12

The Triple Cord: Acts 14:16–17

Anyone who does not permit his exegesis to be dominated and determined by the preconceived notion of common grace will have to admit that one of the strands of the allegedly unbreakable triple cord of which Zwier wrote is hopelessly destroyed. It was not strong at all. It very readily snapped asunder, because it was of his making. He fabricated that particular strand of his triple cord by inserting the word *men* into Psalm 145:9, while according to the context the text plainly required the insertion of the word *creatures*.

The breaking of this one strand makes the cord considerably weaker.

Let us now test the strength of the second strand of this cord. It is also a text that the synod of Kalamazoo quoted to support the first point of common grace. The text is Acts 14:16–17: "Who in times past suffered all nations to walk in their own ways. Nevertheless he left not himself without witness, in that he did good, and gave us rain from heaven, and fruitful seasons, filling our hearts with food and gladness."

The following is Zwier' interpretation of this passage:

> These verses are so clear that they really need no further interpretation. Here we have clear proof for the general

The Triple Cord: Acts 14:16–17

goodness of God over the heathen, whom he did not favor with his special revelation.

Also to them the Lord did not leave himself without witness, the apostle declares. This is the same thought expressed in Romans 1:20: "For the invisible things of him from the creation of the world are clearly seen, being understood by the things that are made, even his eternal power and Godhead; so that they are without excuse." God did not leave himself without witness to the heathen. From heaven he showed them his goodness in giving to all, Gentiles and Jews, rain and fruitful seasons and filling their hearts with food and gladness.

One interpreter justly remarked that God filled our *hearts*, not merely our *stomachs*, so that by his nourishment and providential care his rational creatures could gratefully rejoice in him with their hearts.

Notice further that in the apostle's declaration the sovereignty of God and the responsibility of man are placed side by side, without the slightest attempt to reconcile them for our understanding. The scriptures never do this. But both truths are professed without reservation.

God suffered the heathen to walk in their own ways. In this the apostle clearly evinces the sovereignty of him who does with the host of heaven and the nations of the earth according to his good pleasure. In harmony with his eternal counsel he withheld from the heathen his special revelation and gave them no knowledge of the way of salvation, as he did to Israel.

Yet, even among the heathen God did not leave himself without witness, which reveals the responsibility of man. Because good things—rain, fruitful seasons, food, and gladness—came to them from heaven, even the heathen should have obtained sufficient knowledge of the Creator of heaven and earth to glorify him in his eternal power and Godhead. Therefore, they are without excuse.

To this goodness of God, shown also to the heathen, the apostle draws the attention of his heathen audience. And this statement is the clearest proof for the general goodness as one could wish for. (God's General Goodness, 16)

Just as was the case with Zwier's interpretation of Psalm 145:9, so also here he considers the task of interpreting this text to be extremely easy. In respect to Psalm 145 he remarked that a child could understand it at once. Yet as we have proven, Zwier certainly misunderstood that text. Here we see him again assume the same easy attitude that the text needs no interpretation. I fear that he too easily perceives of his task and takes the matter too lightly. He assumes the same attitude as the synod of 1924 that merely quoted and took for granted that the text is sufficiently clear without interpretation. Such an attitude is dangerous; it causes us to become careless and superficial. Imagining that the text is easily understood, we do not even try to exegete it properly. We simply accept as the proper meaning of the text the surface explanation most in harmony with our notions.

However, Zwier certainly offers an interpretation of the text and inserts something foreign into the sense of it. It would seem that if one is of the opinion that a text is so clear that it needs no interpretation, it would be more proper and to the point simply to let it stand as it is, without inserting anything of our own. But this he does not do. He reads the text as if it conveyed the thought that God bore witness to the heathen and was filled with favor and loving-kindness in regard to them, since he gave them rain and fruitful seasons and filled their hearts with food and gladness. Zwier clearly expresses later in the article quoted above that the word scripture uses in the text denotes benefits that flow from a gracious disposition of God.

If we read in Acts 14:16–17 that the rain and fruitful seasons the heathen received from God were manifestations of a favorable, or gracious, disposition of God toward them, we would not know

The Triple Cord: Acts 14:16–17

how to explain the passage in the light of the rest of the word of God. Certainly the current doctrine of scripture is that God is not gracious to the wicked but remains angry with them forever. In addition, the Bible teaches that rain, sunshine, prosperity, and abundance of earthly things may not be interpreted as evidences of God's gracious disposition toward the reprobate ungodly. If this were the meaning of the text, it would conflict with itself and contain a flat contradiction. The text declares emphatically that God suffered the heathen to walk in their own ways. Those ways were ungodly, iniquity, idolatry, and dissipation, as the apostle pictured them in very dark colors in Romans 1. They were ways in which the heathen rushed into destruction. God suffered them to walk in those ways of corruption and death. He did not put forth his hand to save them. As he revealed himself to Israel, he did not reveal himself to the heathen. With all their food and gladness he suffered the heathen to hasten to their destruction.

This seems to offer no difficulty to Zwier. He does not hesitate to accept such contradictions. He has no difficulty even in reading the text thus: "Although God was filled with loving-kindness toward the heathen nations, he suffered them to rush into destruction." But we do not follow him here. Out of respect for the word of God, we must reject such absurdities. If the text did state that rain and sunshine were a testimony of God concerning his loving-kindness toward the ungodly, we would not know how to explain it.

But that is not the case. Zwier again inserts something into the text and draws a conclusion from it. God does good in giving rain and fruitful seasons to the wicked and filling their hearts with food and gladness. Therefore he is graciously disposed toward them.

We have already proven from other passages of Holy Writ that this conclusion is not warranted. It is possible that God gives rain and fruitful seasons, fills the hearts with food and gladness, causes the wicked to grow as the grass, and all the workers of iniquity to flourish, in order to put them on slippery places and to cast them into destruction. When God does this for the heathen, one certainly cannot conclude that he is favorably disposed toward them. This is evidently the case here, for God suffered the heathen to walk in their ungodly ways to destruction.

Nor is it true, as Zwier seems to think, that the word used in the original Greek of this text denotes a gracious or favorable disposition in God. It cannot be determined with certainty which of two words occurs in the Greek. Essentially it makes no difference because neither denotes a *disposition* in God, but both refer to the *deed* or *work* of the Lord.

Therefore, we deny that Zwier has the right to draw his conclusion. He begs the question. That which he ought to prove, namely, the favorable disposition in God, he carries into the text.

I also disagree with Zwier's exegesis on some points of minor importance.

When we read in Acts 14:17 that God filled not the stomachs, but the "hearts" of the heathen, I do not believe this conveys the meaning that God's purpose was to induce his rational creatures to rejoice in him with grateful hearts. Zwier does not say it in so many words, but he leaves the impression that the divine purpose was to cause those heathen to taste God's grace and loving-kindness and thus to dispose them to gratitude toward him. The result did not correspond to the purpose God had in view. He failed. Apart from being a dangerous doctrine, it conflicts with the plain words of the text: God suffered the heathen to walk in their own ways. It is, however, a simple fact that not a man's stomach but his heart is filled with food and gladness. Hunger is not merely an empty stomach, but a disagreeable sensation and experience, and therefore it really concerns the heart of man. It is not merely the stomach that is filled with food, but man himself, so that his heart is satisfied. That this is the actual meaning of the text is evident from the words "and gladness."

Another point of difference concerns Zwier's presentation of the sovereignty of God and the responsibility of man as running parallel and being mentioned side by side in the text without any apparent relation between them. He presents these truths in that light and is of the opinion that scripture supports his presentation. I do not believe this is true, nor are sovereignty and responsibility presented in Acts 14 as being without any conceivable mutual relation. That there is a certain relation between God's suffering the heathen to walk in their own ways and his giving rain and fruitful seasons is evident from the conjunction "nevertheless." In the Dutch Bible this word is rendered by *ofschoon* (although), which is probably a better translation. The word introduces a concession and prevents the conclusion that might seem to follow from what precedes. The apostle wrote that God suffered the heathen to walk in their own ways. One could conclude that they knew nothing about God and their calling with regard to him. But that was not the case. He did not leave himself without witness. God did not hinder them from walking in their own ways, although he caused himself to be known to them as the good God. And the heathen walked in corruption and ungodliness, although they might have known better.

It is evident that the text requires some explanation.

Emphasis falls on God's suffering the heathen to walk in their own ways. Those ways were in sin and debauchery (Rom. 1). He showed them no grace. He did not save them. He did not reveal himself to them as the God of their salvation. He gave them over to the lusts of their own hearts and flesh. He suffered them to hasten to destruction without putting out a hand to save them. And they would not serve and glorify him.

This does not imply that he gave the heathen no testimony at all concerning himself. He did not leave himself without witness. He plainly manifested that he is the good God, whom we must acknowledge and glorify as such. This testimony was given in his doing good, giving rain from heaven and fruitful seasons, and filling their hearts with food and gladness. In the original there are three participles: doing good, giving, and filling. The first denotes how God gave witness of himself: doing good. The second expresses what his doing good was: giving rain from heaven and fruitful seasons. The last indicates the result for the heathen of God's doing good: their hearts were filled with food and gladness. Their feelings of satisfaction and their gladness therefore could not be attributed to the idols they served, for they came directly from heaven.

These good things they received from heaven were not to be viewed by them as so many Christmas presents through which God testified to them, "Although you are so wicked, I am nevertheless favorably disposed toward you," as Zwier's interpretation implies. But the good things were a testimony of the God of heaven concerning himself, "I am good, the overflowing fountain of all good; you shall love and serve and glorify me and not the idols." As they did not heed that witness, but continued to walk in ways of sin, idolatry and corrupt practices, God was not graciously disposed toward them, but the wrath of God abode on them. This receives all the emphasis in the text. God never leaves himself without witness, whether he saves the sinner or suffers him to walk in his own ways to destruction. Thus we explain this passage. Of a gracious disposition of God toward the ungodly there is no mention at all.

Let us compare this interpretation with Zwier's from the viewpoint of the conception of God implied in each explanation.

Zwier's conception can be expressed as follows: God says to the heathen, "I certainly do not intend to save you, but I suffer you to go to hell. On the way thither I will show you that I am favorably disposed toward you by making your heart glad with food and drink." God suffers the heathen to walk in their own ways, although he is favorably disposed toward them.

According to our interpretation God says to the heathen nations, "I suffer you to walk in your own ways, but even in those ways you must know that I am good and that you ought to glorify and thank me." Our interpretation differs considerably from what Zwier presents to his readers as our explanation.

The Triple Cord: Acts 14:16–17

I called attention to the fact that he never has the courtesy to quote us literally, nor even to refer his readers to passages from our writings so they can check his allegations. He just writes about us in general. He intentionally leaves the impression with his readers that we entertain just one notion: there is no common grace. With this preconceived notion we turn to scripture and so distort its plain words to make them harmonize with our ideas. This one notion we impose on every text.

The same impression he gives of our explanation of Acts 14. It is evident from what he writes that he has not the slightest idea how we really interpret the text. He did not even try to find out, but he proceeded on the assumption that into this text we also carried our own notions.

> The brethren that stumbled in 1924 are, of course, well acquainted with this text. Now, how do they attempt to get themselves out of the difficulty it causes them? They deny, as we know, the general goodness of God. Therefore, this text must somehow be interpreted so there is no mention in it of the general goodness of God toward the heathen nations. Just as with other scriptural passages that speak of God's goodness, or loving-kindness, over the nonelect, they adduce also in this case especially two arguments. They must be examined.
>
> The first argument is briefly as follows: Whatever God does is always good. When he gives rain and fruitful seasons, food and gladness, no matter to whom he gives them, he bestows good things. These gifts are good in themselves, apart from the purpose God may have in mind with them according to his eternal good pleasure. They are revelations of his goodness. But we must distinguish the twofold purpose God has in mind in the bestowal of good things. God does good when he bestows gifts on his elect. In this case his purpose is to bless them through the gifts. All things, prosperity and adversity, work together for good to

them. For them good things are, therefore, a manifestation of God's gracious disposition toward them.

God also does good when he bestows gifts on the heathen. For them the good gifts are not intended as a blessing but as a curse. It is good that he reprobated them. It is also good that he suffers them to walk in their own ways of iniquity. It is good that he gives them things that are intended for their destruction and that through these things he causes them to become ripe for judgment.

What God does, therefore, is always good. And in this sense we must understand the words of the apostle Paul, when he tells his heathen audience at Lystra that God did good from heaven by giving them rain and fruitful seasons and filling their hearts with food and gladness. (God's General Goodness, 16)

Zwier then proceeds to show why this exegesis is unacceptable. His opinion is that there is an element of truth in our argumentation, "but as an interpretation of this particular text it must decidedly be rejected" (God's General Goodness, 16).

With this last opinion of his we wholeheartedly agree. Whoever would offer the above alleged argumentation as an interpretation of Acts 14 would thereby reveal that he did not understand the first rules of interpretation. However much I regret that I must write this in public, the truth must be said, and the truth is that Zwier commits the sin of a downright lie when he informs his readers that we have interpreted the text as he presents it. As a man, and especially as a Christian, he ought to do one of two things: either prove that we ever offered in our writings his alleged explanation of Acts 14:16–17 or acknowledge that he slandered us. Convinced I am that he cannot do the former. Nowhere can he find where we offered the argumentation he presents above as an interpretation of this text. He simply invented this story.

More than once we interpreted this text, and gladly I will help

The Triple Cord: Acts 14:16–17

Zwier find the passages in our writings where our interpretation can be found. He can find them in the *Standard Bearer* (2:2, 23, 321; 9:404). I will not copy those passages here. However, I kindly ask Zwier to do that in *De Wachter* and thus remove the very bad impression concerning our way of handling the word of God that his readers must have received through his deceptive presentation of our interpretation of this text.

The second argument we usually adduce and apply in this case, according to Zwier, is the appeal to Psalm 73 and Psalm 92. To appeal to other passages of scripture to interpret a given text is perfectly legitimate. We certainly are not ashamed to say that we interpret the Bible in its own light, and Zwier may not deprecate this method. But the fact is that on this point Zwier also does not write the truth. I do not believe he can refer his readers to a single passage from our writings where we appealed to these psalms to explain Acts 14:16–17. He again invents a story.

The interpretation we always gave of this text is the same one we offer in this chapter, and this interpretation we still maintain against Zwier's. Wholly in agreement with all the rest of Holy Writ, Acts 14:16–17 teaches that God does good from heaven. In his doing good, in his giving rain and fruitful seasons and filling men's hearts with food and gladness, there is a testimony of God concerning himself. Although this testimony is not as clear and rich as that of God's revelation in Christ and also has a different character, it places man before the divine demand to serve and to glorify God and to turn away from idols and corruption. If God, together with this witness of himself, does not give grace to man, man will continue in his sinful ways. This is no evidence of God's favorable disposition at all.

This cuts the second strand of Zwier's triple cord.

Chapter 13

The Triple Cord: Luke 6:35

It must be admitted that two of the threads that constitute the triple cord of which Zwier speaks could not stand the test of sound exegesis and are hopelessly broken, and the strong triple cord exists no longer. Only one of the threads is left, and its strength must now be tested.

This last thread is Luke 6:35 in connection with Matthew 5:45. "Love ye your enemies, and do good, and lend, hoping for nothing again; and your reward shall be great, and ye shall be the children of the Highest: for he is kind unto the unthankful and to the evil" (Luke 6:35).

Zwier, taking his task too lightly, even as he did with the other two passages, writes about Luke 6:35 as follows:

> Also this passage from scripture is so clear, that we really deplore that we are obliged to waste paper and ink to the cause of explaining it. The simple quotation of this text from the sermon on the mount ought to be sufficient, as was considered sufficient by the synod of 1924. One who reads this text in its connection immediately realizes that the only possible interpretation is that God is merciful to his enemies, the unthankful and evil. (God's General Goodness, 17)

The Triple Cord: Luke 6:35

With this we can agree. Another explanation is out of the question, because what Zwier offers is no explanation at all, but only a repetition of the text. If he does not say anything else about this passage, he and I can certainly agree regarding its meaning. For we also hold that it teaches that God is merciful to his enemies, the unthankful and evil.

But this cannot be the last word about this passage, as everyone immediately feels. Even though Zwier does not think it worthwhile to waste paper and ink to explain this passage, we will have to regard our task a little more seriously. The questions arise at once: Who are these enemies to whom God is merciful and kind? What is meant by the kindness of God? To these questions Zwier immediately replies, "All unthankful and evil are mentioned in one breath in the text. The text does not distinguish between elect and reprobate. God's kindness is nonsaving grace and therefore refers to God's common grace. He is kind to all the unthankful and evil."

The reader will see immediately that Zwier inserts something that is not in the text. He does not quote the text literally, but offers an interpretation and makes an important change. Just as in Psalm 145:9 he inserted the word *men* and in Acts 14:16–17 he inserted the *favorable disposition* of God, so in Luke 6 he inserts the word *all*. The text does not speak of *all* the unthankful and evil. Nor must we be too hasty to argue that it speaks of unthankful and evil without further limitation and that, therefore, *all* the unthankful and evil are meant. It appears that Zwier follows this line of argumentation. His opinion is that this interpretation is corroborated by a comparison between Luke 6:35 and Matthew 5:45.

This is a very dangerous method. Apart from the fact that such an interpretation does not consider at all the current teaching of scripture concerning God's attitude toward the reprobate ungodly, it is quite improper to read Luke 6:35 as if it referred to all the ungodly, merely on the basis that they are not further defined. If this method of interpretation were sound in this instance, it certainly must be applied in all other cases. That is, wherever the Bible speaks of the ungodly without any limitation, we must insert the word *all*. If we would apply this method to similar passages of the word of God, we would conclude that the Arminian doctrine that Christ died for all men is correct.

Zwier, in interpreting the text in Luke, will have nothing of any limitation. "Unthankful and evil" according to him are all men without distinction. In his opinion it is certain that the text does not refer to the elect unthankful and evil. He writes the following concerning his objections against what he thinks is our interpretation of the text:

> Is it necessary at all to repudiate this interpretation?
>
> It must be clear to anyone who is not controlled by prejudice that we have to do here with the worst example of perverting scripture. This is no explanation of the words of Jesus, but an induction of one's notions into the text. Arbitrarily something that is not contained in the text is inserted. For the text does not say that God shows kindness to those who *formerly* were unthankful and evil, but are now converted from their unthankfulness and wickedness. Nor do we read here that God is kind to those who still are unthankful and evil, but will be converted from their unthankfulness and wickedness in the future. This is made of the text, but it does not say this. This arbitrary, high-handed exegesis is the result of dogmatic prejudice. (God's General Goodness, 17)

The error and danger of this exegetical method, which refuses to interpret scripture in its own light and is satisfied with explaining each individual text by itself, become apparent when we apply it to other parts of Holy Writ. Just apply it to Romans 5:6: "For when we were yet without strength, in due time Christ died for the ungodly." The result is that you will reason as follows: The text says that Christ died for the ungodly. It does not say that Christ died for those who *formerly* were ungodly, but now are no longer ungodly. Neither

The Triple Cord: Luke 6:35

does the text teach that Christ died for those who at that time were still ungodly, but would be converted from their ungodliness. The text speaks wholly in general of the ungodly. Therefore, one has no right to insert the word *elect* into the text. One who limits the text to the elect ungodly is guilty of perverting the word of God, for the passage teaches clearly that Christ died for *all* the ungodly.

We know very well that in this case Zwier would not reason thus. He would not apply the same method to interpret Romans 5:6 that he follows in his explanation of Luke 6:35. He would object that the word of God elsewhere teaches plainly that Christ did not die for all men but only for the elect; that we must remember this in the interpretation of Romans 5:6; and that the true explanation of the Romans passage cannot be that Christ died for all men. But this is arbitrary. You cannot apply two completely different methods of interpretation to scripture. Yet this is precisely what Zwier does.

If we would follow the same method to interpret Luke 6:35 that he admits is the correct method with application to Romans 5:6, he would suddenly face about and brand that method as a perversion of scripture and the result of dogmatic prejudice. Then he would deny us the right to limit the unthankful and evil to the elect only, although there is nothing in the text or context that forbids such an interpretation, and it harmonizes with the correct teaching of the word of God throughout. Then Zwier would not hesitate to insert the word *all* into the text.

Zwier's opinion is that his interpretation of Luke 6:35 is corroborated by Matthew 5:45. The Matthew passage, which teaches that God makes his sun to rise on the evil and on the good and sends rain on the just and on the unjust, sheds light on Luke 6:35. If you compare the two passages and explain one in the light of the other, your conclusion must be that the Luke text teaches that God is kind to *all* the unthankful and evil. The sun rises on *all men*, and the rain descends from heaven on *all*. It is also evident that Matthew 5:45 signifies that in causing his sun to rise and the rain to fall on all men, God reveals his kindness and graciousness to all. Because he loves all men, he causes his sun to rise on all and sends rain to all.

The matter appears to be simple. The text in Matthew presents to Zwier no difficulties whatever. That is usually the case with those who are satisfied with explaining each text by itself and not considering the current teaching of scripture.

Yet the matter is not as easy as it appears. We have clearly and abundantly shown that according to the current teaching of the Bible, we may not consider earthly things *per se*—rain and sunshine and riches and prosperity—as proofs of God's love and grace with respect to the reprobate ungodly. On the contrary, they are slippery places on which God causes them to fall into eternal destruction. The ungodly flourish in order to be destroyed forever. When we remember this, we are inclined to look at Matthew 5:24 more closely before we accept with Zwier that it teaches that rain and sunshine are manifestations of God's gracious disposition to all the ungodly. When we study the text more closely and in its context, our objection to Zwier's interpretation becomes more serious. In Matthew 5:44 we read, "Love your enemies, bless them that curse you, do good to them that hate you, and pray for them which despitefully use you, and persecute you." We are exhorted to do these things to our enemies because we must follow the example of our heavenly Father: "that ye may be the children of your Father which is in heaven: for he maketh his sun to rise on the evil and on the good, and sendeth rain on the just and on the unjust" (v. 45). If we take the text in its context, it means that we must love our enemies *because* and *even as* God loves his enemies. We must really love them, seek their real good, bless them, pray for them, and seek their salvation, even as God really loves them, seeks their good, and saves them to the very end. Zwier may have no difficulty here and no objection to letting the text teach that God thus loves all his enemies, but we maintain that the whole of the word of God militates against that interpretation.

The Triple Cord: Luke 6:35

Besides, we must not forget that sunshine and rain are not always blessings. Sometimes the sun causes a scorching heat, and crops dry up and wither. When rain is too abundant, everything rots in the field. Also then God causes his sun to shine and the rain to fall on the just and on the unjust alike, and to both he also sends hail and fire, earthquakes and destruction, and pestilence and death.

At the most we can say that Matthew 5:44–45 refer to God's providential care in sending rain and causing his sun to shine on the just and the unjust as examples for the children of God to follow. When in this dispensation God sends good gifts and means to men, he does not limit them to the righteous, but he sends them promiscuously to the godly and to the ungodly, to the just and to the unjust alike. He does not leave himself without witness. This is revealed in its most general form in rain and sunshine. With the rain and sunshine comes the calling and obligation to glorify the living God and to give thanks to him who does all these things. When this is done by the righteous man, he receives favor and blessing from God. When the ungodly man fails to give God the glory, he receives no blessing, nor is he the object of God's favor, even though he receives rain and sunshine. The wrath of God abides on him. The child of God, who must be perfect even as his Father in heaven is perfect, must follow his example in this. He received the love of God and experienced and tasted that love of God as a love to his enemies. Because he also was God's enemy even as others, he must manifest this love to his enemies. He must not greet only those who greet him and bless those who bless him, but he must do good to all, even to his enemies. He cannot reveal this love of God by loving the enemies of God and having fellowship with them, but he must do good to them by telling them the truth, by blessing them and praying for them, and by showing them the way of life. He must not hate those who hate him, and never must he avenge himself by doing evil to his enemies, for then he would not manifest the love of God, but the sinful love of the ungodly. He must be a child of his Father in heaven and be perfect. The most general example of this he can see in God's causing his sun to rise and the rain to descend on the just and the unjust in common. And did he not cause Christ to die in due time for the ungodly? Of a gracious disposition to every man, particularly to the reprobate ungodly, there is no mention at all in Matthew 5:44–45.

We still maintain the interpretation we always offered of this passage, and which we will repeat here because Zwier does not correctly present it to his readers. It is found in the *Standard Bearer* (1:20–21). The quotation is from an article written by Henry Danhof:

> Both texts [Matt. 5:44-45; Luke 6:35] have the same tendency and purpose. They would have the believers be followers of God as dear children. Their love also they must bring into practice according to the example of God. This thought is expressed in both passages in almost the same words. We have here a part of the sermon on the mount, in which Christ teaches his disciples how they must conduct themselves according to the precepts of his kingdom, written by the Spirit in their hearts. Christ's followers must not walk and act as the ungodly, but must be like their Father who is in heaven. The example he gives they must follow. Such is the thought. This is admitted by all and is evident from the words of Jesus, "I say unto you, Love your enemies, bless them that curse you, do good to them that hate you, and pray for them which despitefully use you, and persecute you; that ye may be the children of your Father which is in heaven: for he maketh his sun to rise on the evil and on the good, and sendeth rain on the just and on the unjust" (Matt. 5:44–45). "Love ye your enemies, and do good, and lend, hoping for nothing again; and your reward shall be great, and ye shall be the children of the Highest: for he is kind unto the unthankful and to the evil" (Luke 6:35).
>
> All the other elements in these passages are subordinate

to this main thought, and we may pass them by for the present to attend to the main questions in these declarations of Jesus. What does God do according to these words? In what must we imitate him? In answering these questions we must be careful lest we turn the order of the two elements around. The synod proceeded from the thought that God loves all his enemies, also the reprobate, because Christ would have his disciples love their enemies. In this way synod arrived at the conclusion that God shows a certain grace, or favor, to the reprobate.

That this method of reasoning is erroneous is evident. We would have the right to draw such a conclusion if the texts mentioned a twofold love of God. Such a conclusion would be permissible if these passages spoke of the love of God for his elect from eternity, according to which he draws them in time with cords of loving-kindness; and of another love of God, in distinction from and in contrast to the love mentioned above, that he shows to his creatures in general, specifically to the reprobate. But the text speaks of only one love of God.

According to these passages, Christ notices among men two different kinds of love. Ungodly and sinners do love, and the disciples of Jesus must also love. Now it is the will of Christ that there is an essential difference between the love of the ungodly and the love of his disciples. Sinners love sinners, those who are like them, with the purpose of receiving from them. Therefore, their love in its deepest root is only selfishness. It is not real love. According to the standard of this love, which is no love, the love of the disciples may not manifest itself.

The children of the kingdom must love as God loves, and God's love is more than the love of sinners. They can only love those who love them; their enemies they are unable to love. But God is able to love his enemies. If this were not the case, we would all be lost, for by nature we are all enemies of God. God is able to love those who do not love him. From this viewpoint is implied the possibility of our salvation. God loved us while we were yet his enemies. Therefore, we can now also love. Our love harmonizes with God's love. Through the love of God we are able to love our enemies. In this we excel the unregenerate.

That this is the correct conception of the texts is manifest from the contexts of both Matthew and Luke. Nowhere do these passages speak of a twofold love of God, the love of God to the elect and another love to the reprobate. Throughout the love of Jesus' disciples is contrasted with the conception of "those of old time" and with the love of sinners. Their righteousness must be greater than that of the scribes, and only then are they blessed when men hate them, separate them, revile them, and reject their names as evil for the sake of the Son of man. The love of sinners, therefore, must be manifested as hate with respect to Jesus' disciples.

Therefore, Jesus does not hesitate one moment to condemn the love of sinners. This would have been absurd if it had been his intention to teach that the Father also loves his reprobate enemies, and that sinners do really love, and that the disciples must also love sinners who are enemies of God. In that case Jesus' act would have directly contradicted his instruction to his disciples and the example of God.

The thought here is that his disciples must not love as sinners love, for they do not truly love, but they must love as the Father loves. They must be perfect, even as their Father in heaven is perfect.

This was our interpretation at the very beginning of our controversy. And this interpretation makes a completely different impression than the impression Zwier intended to present to his readers as our explanation of these passages. Contemptuously he wrote the following:

> Now, notice how they try to save themselves out of the difficulty! They say that Jesus by "the unthankful and evil" refers to God's elect people. For, also we are by nature all unthankful and in principle enemies of God. And God is filled with eternal loving-kindness toward those unthankful and evil, whom he chose unto eternal life, and he loved them while they were still enemies. Toward them he is so merciful that he causes all things, also the rain and the sunshine, to work for their good. But it is loving-kindness that works for good only for his people, even while they are still unthankful and evil. This is their interpretation of this text.

He evidently did not investigate and read our exegesis, and he preferred not to quote us literally. Here and everywhere he simply proceeds from the assumption that we have a certain preconceived dogmatic notion and that wherever scripture does not agree with this notion, we simply carry it into the text. I do not understand what right he thought he had to proceed from such an assumption. Certain it is that he can find no ground for it in our writings. Anyone who does not simply take for granted that Zwier writes the truth, but investigates for himself, will have to admit that we are not guilty of committing the fundamental error he attributes to us. We have always emphasized the necessity of interpreting the word of God in the light of its own context and of its current teaching. This principle we also applied to the texts in Matthew and Luke. When the passages are interpreted according to this sound method, the following elements appear on the foreground as the true meaning of the texts.

First, God revealed his love and caused his people to know and to taste that love as love that is capable of being merciful and kind to his enemies. This is the only love of God mentioned in the texts and in their contexts.

Second, the children of God, in whose hearts this love of God is poured out, and who experience and taste this love of God as a love to their enemies, must manifest this love in their lives and walk in the world. Hence they must love not only those who love them, but also their enemies who revile and persecute them. They must do good to them, pray for them, and bless them. In doing this they manifest the image of their Father in heaven.

Third, as a most general example of this they must look at God's work in nature, where he causes his sun to rise on the evil and on the good and sends rain on the just and on the unjust.

But of a certain grace, or favor, of God toward the reprobate ungodly these two passages speak not at all.

It is Zwier's right and privilege to differ with us and to offer his interpretation. But let him be honest regarding us and correctly present our explanation of the texts. Let him also offer an explanation and not simply state that the passages are very clear and need no exegesis. If he would attempt to exegete them, he would soon find that he meets with insurmountable difficulties and that there are serious objections against his meaning of these passages. The passages certainly exhort us truly to love our enemies. This does not mean that in a general sense we must be nice to them in regard to temporal things, but that we must love them to the end, bless them, and pray for them. If in this we must be children of our Father in heaven and reflect his love, which, it must be admitted, is always infinitely greater and more perfect than ours, it follows that he also loves his enemies to the end, answers our prayers when we pray for them, blesses them, and saves them. How could Zwier possibly apply this to all men, specifically to the reprobate ungodly?

He would soon have to admit that his interpretation is untenable in the light of the contexts and of scripture in general.

So I conclude that the entire triple cord, of which Zwier boasted that it could not be broken, is completely destroyed.

Chapter 14

Goodness That Leads to Repentance

As a faithful son of the Christian Reformed Church, Zwier, in support of his contention that there is a general goodness, or grace, of God, appeals to all those passages to which the synod of Kalamazoo in 1924 also referred to prove the first point of common grace.

He also remains faithful to this church when he offers the same exegesis of those texts that the 1924 synod suggested when it referenced the texts in support of the first point. The synod did not attempt any exegesis of the texts, but what the synod conceived to be its interpretation of them is plain from the use synod made of the texts.

I am seriously inclined to doubt whether Zwier's exegesis is entirely free from those influences that may never dominate exegesis of scripture. If he had not conceived it to be his calling to defend the three points, but to let the truth have its free course and to shed light on the matter of common grace, regardless of the declarations of the synod of Kalamazoo, his interpretation of some of the scripture passages might have been quite different. As matters stand, he serves his own denomination of churches but not *the church*; he defends certain theories but not the truth. He repeatedly asseverates that he hates to thresh old straw, but in reality he does nothing else.

This also applies to his interpretation of Romans 2:4, discussed in chapter 7.

The straw he threshes in explaining this text as he does is very old. Pelagians and semi-Pelagians always employed this text to attack those who defended the truth of God's sovereign grace. Striking it is that Zwier explains this text in the same way and uses it to the same purpose as those enemies of the Reformed truth. This ought to make him reflect on and to review his interpretation, especially since he denies the accusation that he shows Arminian tendencies in the development of his theory of God's general goodness. The heretic Julian appealed to this text against Augustine and explained it as teaching a general goodness of God to lead all men to repentance. As far as God's intention is concerned, he is willing to save all men. If some are not saved, the ultimate cause must not be sought in God's unwillingness to save them, or because his general loving-kindness did not include all men, but in their rejection of his saving mercy. Augustine's interpretation was quite different. He replied that God's goodness certainly leads to repentance, but only for those whom he predestinated. With regard to the others, Augustine wrote that not one of them does God lead to saving and spiritual repentance. God is and remains perfectly sovereign (Augustine, *Contra Julianum*, 5:14; A. D. R. Polman, *De Predestinatieleer van Augustinus*, 94).

Zwier attacks Augustine's interpretation and will have nothing of our interpretation that the goodness of God concerns only the elect. It is evident from what he writes that he does not know our exegesis and did not investigate what we wrote on the matter. He proceeds on the assumption that everywhere we deliberately attempt to bring scripture into harmony with our preconceived notions. He will have nothing of the interpretation that God's goodness that leads to repentance concerns only those whom he has chosen unto eternal life. He agrees with all the heretics who used this text to oppose the defenders of God's sovereign grace and explained the goodness of God as including all men.

Goodness That Leads to Repentance

Prof. Louis Berkhof did the same in his pamphlet *The Three Points*. According to his interpretation, Romans 2:4 expresses God's intention to lead the ungodly Jews to repentance, but the result did not correspond to God's purposes.

Yet the brethren assert that they show no Arminian tendencies.

Zwier's opinion is that in the context the apostle Paul does not address man in general but particularly the Jews.

If, however, this conception is correct, we have, strictly speaking, no proof in the text for the goodness of God in the most general sense. For, if the Jew is addressed, the question of the apostle, "Or despisest thou the riches of his goodness and forbearance and longsuffering?" cannot refer to general blessings in the sense that all men share them. The latter is, indeed, true of the blessings of which we spoke in our former articles, rain and fruitful seasons and food and gladness. All men receive these good gifts of God, heathen as well as Jews, the evil as well as the good, the unrighteous as well as the righteous, and in them God reveals his general goodness. But to Israel he gave many blessings that he withheld from the heathen.

Later in the chapter the apostle refers to that: "Behold, thou art called a Jew, and restest in the law, and makest thy boast of God, and knowest his will, and approvest the things that are more excellent, being instructed out of the law" (vv. 17–18). And he refers to that in chapter 6:1–2: "What advantage then hath the Jew? or what profit is there of circumcision? Much every way; chiefly because that unto them were committed the oracles of God."

Undoubtedly the apostle refers to those covenantal blessings in his question whether the Jew despises the riches of God's goodness. This is what we call a rhetorical question: the answer is implied in it. The Jew whom the apostle addresses, indeed, despised the riches of God's goodness, long-suffering, and forbearance. He boasted of the privileges that as a son of Abraham he received. He concluded from them that all was well with him and that he was righteous before God, since he was so richly blessed by God. Proudly he condemned the heathen, whose judge he presumed to be. And the apostle tells him all this in clear language. Instead of suffering yourself to be led unto repentance by the goodness of God, after the hardness of your impenitent heart you gather unto yourself wrath against the day of wrath and revelation of the righteous judgment of God, who will render to every man according to his works.

It becomes clearly evident, therefore, from this text that God shows his goodness also to those who contemn and despise it and thus gather to themselves treasures in the place of destruction. It is the same truth found in the sermon on the mount, that God is kind to the unthankful and the evil.

Even though according to this conception the text cannot serve as proof for the goodness of God in the most general sense, because not all men share in the blessings meant here, still it follows from the text that God's goodness is not limited to the elect. Nonelect also share God's goodness. So much is clear, is it not?

The synod of 1924 could, therefore, justly appeal to this text.

To correctly understand Zwier's interpretation of this text, it is not superfluous to note his objections against the interpretation that limits the goodness of God to the elect only.

The untenableness of this conception, which we pointed out before, becomes clearly manifest here too. Anyone who reads the text without prejudice immediately feels that the apostle proceeds from the thought that every day God was still blessing the despisers of his goodness. The apostle

Goodness That Leads to Repentance

does not say to them, "You make a mistake; these blessings are essentially curses that God sends down on your heads." But he points them to the fact that God still continually causes them to share in the riches of his goodness. In this the Jews did not err. But they erred in concluding from God's goodness that it was well with them and that they were righteous in the eyes of God. This sweet dream the apostle disturbs with the declaration that they were gathering unto themselves treasures of wrath in hell.

From Zwier's viewpoint the Jews had plenty of reason for this "sweet dream." There was a treasure of divine goodness for those ungodly Jews, which was proof of an equally rich disposition of favor and grace in God concerning them. And then the Jews still erred when they thought all was well with them? What a strange argumentation is that of Zwier. I cannot understand his conception of the riches of God's goodness!

We must follow him just a little farther. He writes that we still have another "little argument," which must take a moment to enervate.

They say that the text speaks of God's goodness *that leads to repentance,* and this must certainly refer to saving goodness. For only the elect are thus led to repentance by the goodness of God. Never does it lead one other to repentance. Therefore, we certainly must limit this goodness of God to the mercy that he shows only to the elect.

It is not difficult to refute this interpretation.

Just note that the brethren do not correctly quote the apostle. They make him say something that he does not say. Rather, they omit something he does say.

[The reader must remember that Zwier never quotes us literally. He simply ascribes many errors to us, he does not care which. We meet here again one of these downright untruths that permeate his articles.]

If Paul actually said here that the goodness of God leads to repentance, this interpretation might pass muster. Then we might understand this text as referring to the saving goodness of God toward the elect, for they, and they only, are led to repentance by it. But the brethren, we trust unintentionally, omit a little word here. The apostle writes that the goodness of God leads "thee" to repentance. He addresses the ungodly Jew, the despiser of the riches of his goodness, who after his hardness and impenitent heart gathers unto himself wrath in the day of wrath and revelation of the righteous judgment of God. To him Paul addresses his question: "Knowest thou not that the goodness of God leadeth thee to repentance?" Hence it is impossible to think that the apostle refers to the saving goodness of God, for in it only the elect share, and they are surely being led by it to repentance.

The apostle has in mind a certain goodness of God that does, indeed, lead to repentance; that is, that has that tendency, or as the marginal notes of our *Statenbijbel* have it, that give you time and reasons to repent, but that never actually leads the object of this goodness to true repentance.

I briefly summarize Zwier's interpretation of this text.

First, the riches of the goodness of God were for the Jews, in distinction from the heathen. The Jews had many benefits and blessings, such as the word of God, the covenants, the law and the shadows, temple, altar, priest, sacrifice, and the like. These privileges were blessings for every Jew, head for head, and were intended by God to be blessings for the Jews.

Second, those blessings and benefits were proofs of the favorable disposition of God toward every Jew without distinction and exception. That this is Zwier's interpretation is plain from his writings quoted above and his intention to prove the truth of the first point from this text, just as the synod of 1924 did. God proved in all these things that he was favorably disposed to all the Jews.

Third, the tendency and purpose of those benefits and privileges was to lead all Jews to repentance. That was the end of the riches of God's goodness. If we do not play with words, this must mean that God in his great goodness sought to lead all the Jews to conversion and repentance. If this is not the meaning of Zwier's explanation of the text, I would like him to explain himself clearly. As I understand him at present, he teaches that there was in God a merciful will to lead every Jew to repentance and salvation.

Fourth, that goodness of God is not saving goodness. This means that although God had intended that goodness to be saving, it did not have the desired and purposed result. The Jews resisted that goodness of God, hardened themselves, and thus gathered to themselves treasures of wrath. The goodness of God is therefore resistible.

Zwier's teaching is the doctrine of the semi-Pelagians. He may insist ever so emphatically that he is soundly Reformed and that with us he condemns Arminianism. But I confidently declare that anyone who is able to pass a Reformed judgment on this matter must admit that with his interpretation of Romans 2:4 Zwier landed in the camp of the enemy of the Reformed truth, just as Berkhof did.

Let us assume that Zwier has the right to change the clear words of the text as he does. The words "goodness of God that leadeth thee to repentance" are changed into "goodness of God that has the tendency to bring thee to convert thyself, but that will never actually lead thee to repentance." To express the matter briefly and succinctly, he changes the words "that leadeth thee to repentance" into their opposite: "that never will lead thee to repentance." These are his words: "The apostle has in mind a certain goodness of God… that never actually leads the object of this goodness to repentance."

However, the text speaks of a goodness that leads to repentance. For the sake of argument let us assume that this change is permissible. In that case God's goodness *tends* to lead men to repentance. But a general goodness of God cannot have this tendency, for it is a goodness of God over righteous and unrighteous, the just and unjust alike. Whether one is righteous or ungodly makes no difference with respect to the goodness of God. General goodness does not cause the testimony to go forth to men, "You must repent in order to share in my goodness." The opposite is true. The general goodness of God declares, "It makes no difference whether or not you repent, I am still filled with loving-kindness toward you." Such goodness cannot have the tendency to lead man to repentance. I would like to have Zwier make clear how it could possibly have such a tendency. If the revelation of the goodness of God has the tendency to lead man to repentance, its content must be particular. From its revelation the testimony must clearly proceed, "I am gracious to the righteous, I love the one who repents. Repent, therefore, and I will be merciful to you and abundantly pardon your iniquities."

Further, Zwier must admit that the benefits and privileges that Israel possessed did not reveal to the Jew such a general goodness of God. The law and the prophets did not proclaim that God was mercifully disposed to every Jew, whether he repented or not. The opposite is true. The law could curse terribly, and the prophets did not proclaim a general goodness of God, but a goodness that was only toward the righteous. And the psalms sing of that particular goodness of Jehovah, loudly proclaiming wrath and damnation on all ungodly Jews.

If we interpret the text so that the expression "goodness of God that leadeth thee to repentance" means goodness of God that has the tendency to lead thee to repentance, then in all the law and the prophets, in all the "advantage" of the Jew, always a particular goodness of God was proclaimed to the Jew—the truth that God is good and gracious only to the righteous.

In this case Zwier is entirely forgetful of his definition of the goodness of God as his self-desirability. But exactly because this is true, God's goodness can be only for the righteous. He can be kind to the unthankful and evil, but then only to the elect unthankful and evil, eternally beheld by him as righteous in Christ. Outside of Christ there is no mercy of God, because God's goodness is for the righteous alone. Those elect sinners, eternally beheld by him in Christ as justified, are called to repentance through the revelation of God's goodness in the law and the prophets and in the gospel. Through his almighty and irresistible grace they are also effectually led to repentance. The goodness of God leads its objects to repentance.

But among Israel there were also the wicked reprobates. Not all was Israel that was of Israel. They also shared the "advantage" of the Jew. They also were witnesses that God is good to the righteous. They beheld it with their eyes. They heard of it with their ears. But they must have nothing of a goodness of God toward the righteous. They plainly saw the goodness of God that leads to repentance, but they despised it. In that way and wholly in harmony with God's purpose, they gathered to themselves treasures of wrath in the day of wrath and revelation of the righteous judgment of God. The meaning of the apostle's question is, do you belong to those who despise the riches of that goodness of God?

This is essentially the interpretation we always offered of this text, except that we were of the opinion that the words "leadeth thee to repentance" are too positive to permit the interpretation of "has the tendency to lead thee to repentance."

Nor is it true, as Zwier alleges, that we omitted the little word "thee." Rather, we were of the opinion that "thee" refers to "man" in Romans 2:1 and that the context does not permit us to limit the first part of this chapter to Jews only. The apostle there speaks of "man, whosoever thou art that judgest." Danhof's interpretation applies the word to the Jews. I prefer to apply it to man in general.

Essentially this does not make the least difference with respect to the question we are now discussing. Whether you refer "thee" to man in general or to the Jew in particular, the goodness of God very really leads to repentance. However, this never concerns the reprobate shell, but always and only the elect kernel. The reprobate Jew despised the goodness of God, which he beheld with his eyes that it led the elect Jew to repentance. The reprobate Jew would not repent. He loved the darkness rather than the light. That impenitent Jew certainly was no object of the goodness of God. On the contrary, he gathered to himself treasures of wrath in the day of wrath and revelation of the righteous judgment of God (Rom. 2:5).

From whatever angle you view the matter and whether you speak of the goodness of God that actually leads to repentance, or if you prefer to speak of the goodness of God that has the tendency to lead to repentance, the goodness of God of which the text speaks is assuredly saving goodness, is certainly particular, for the elect only, and is always despised by the reprobate ungodly who witnesses this goodness, so that he gathers to himself treasures of wrath. All this takes place according to the determinate counsel and foreknowledge of God, who is in the heavens and accomplishes all his good pleasure.

But Zwier's interpretation does not fit the text and is essentially that of all Pelagians and semi-Pelagians, who always opposed the Reformed truth.

For the wellbeing of the Reformed churches in our land I earnestly hope that he will repent of his error.

By now it will have become plain to the reader that Romans 2:4 cannot be quoted in support of the theory that God is good to the righteous and to the unrighteous alike.

Chapter 15

Grace without Fruits of Righteousness

In the comparison between Zwier's interpretation of some texts that he imagines support the three points of 1924 and our interpretation of them, we must call attention to what he writes about Isaiah 26:10: "Let favour be shewed to the wicked, yet will he not learn righteousness: in the land of uprightness will he deal unjustly, and will not behold the majesty of the Lord."

I must call attention to an interpretation that Zwier alleges to be ours, although also in this instance he gives no references. I maintain that we never offered the following interpretation:

> It is well known that the opponents of common grace have sometimes attempted to eliminate the word *grace* from this text and that for this idea they appeal to the English translation, in which not *grace* but "favour" is used. [Instead of the expression "let favour be shown to the wicked," a translation of the Dutch is "let grace be shown to the wicked."] They cling to the English translation and imagine to find support for their conception in it. This declaration of the prophet does not speak of grace but of favor.
>
> Now we may admit that this translation is permissible. "Favour" has a wider meaning than grace, but it expresses the meaning of the original quite correctly, and the prophet's

thought remains essentially the same. Yet it appears to me, that *grace* is the correct term to be used here. I am not an Old Testament scholar and do not know so very much of the Hebrew. But the same word that appears here is, as far as I know, everywhere else in the Old Testament translated as "grace," and I see no reason to depart from this translation here. Hence, I rather abide by the opinion of the great majority of scholars from the past and of recent date who also translate the word as "grace." (God's General Goodness, 7)

We have here another proof that Zwier easily attributes to his opponents an opinion that is not theirs. He simply writes, "It is well known." Then he attributes to us the most foolish thing that we appeal to an English translation to determine an exegetical question. It would not surprise us if soon it also will become "well known" that we consider the English translation to be the original. Zwier does not even control his own writing and refer to the passage where we are supposed to have written anything like the above. He does not seem to care whether he writes the truth or the lie about us. If he had looked for proof for what he wrote concerning our exegesis of this text, his effort would have been in vain. It is no wonder that all sorts of foolish notions concerning us are spread among the people and that they believe the stories told them by their leaders such as Zwier.

It comforts us, however, that it is so evident that Zwier is inventing things that any reader who thinks for himself will have noticed it. It must certainly be known that we make no essential distinction between *favor* and *grace*. Zwier knows this too. An appeal to the English translation suits his notions, not ours. It is he who speaks of general goodness rather than of general grace. To us this distinction has no significance. Whether in Isaiah 26:10 you translate "let *grace* be shown to the wicked" or "let *favour* be shown to the wicked" is of no significance to us at all. We gladly admit that the word *grace* is a suitable translation of the text. Never did we try to deny this.

Grace without Fruits of Righteousness

We will therefore pay no further attention to this.

It is a rather self-humiliating confession for a writer on dogmatic subjects who for more than twenty-five years has labored with the scriptures to admit that he does not know very much of the original Hebrew. This may help us understand why he does not make a single attempt to read and interpret Isaiah 26:10 in its proper context. He writes that it is not necessary to write an elaborate treatise on this text. He cannot express it better than it is explained in the *Brief Commentary* by Herman N. Ridderbos, and therefore he simply adopts his interpretation.

Ridderbos translates Isaiah 26:10 as follows: "If the wicked is treated graciously, he learns no righteousness; in a land of uprightness he deals crookedly, and does not behold the majesty of the Lord." The interpretation of Ridderbos, adopted by Zwier, is as follows:

> Placed on the foreground is that God makes the path of the righteous plain. This does not mean that the path is always an easy task, but it means that one does not stumble thereon and, therefore, the final destination is reached. In accordance with this faith the praying prophet expects, together with the righteous whom he represents in his prayer, that the Lord will come in the way of his judgments, to punish his enemies and to redeem his people. It is the intense longing of the devout that God's name and praise may be known and, therefore, in the way of his judgments he may glorify his name and enhance his praise. After this God the praying prophet longs with everything in him and even in the hours of the night. For these judgments are salutary, since they often lead men to the knowledge and practice of righteousness and to repentance. This does not take place when the wicked is always spared, for then he will harden himself in his wickedness. Even in a land where everything is governed according to righteousness and is ordained according to God's law (as in Israel's best periods), the wicked cannot

be persuaded to do the good, but he acts crookedly and perversely because he is blind to the majesty of the Lord.

Ridderbos' interpretation of is quite different from Zwier's, in spite of his contention that he agrees with Ridderbos. It is still an open question how to explain that the period during which the wicked among Israel were spared could be so prolonged. Why was the ungodly man spared? Why was grace, or favor, shown to the wicked? What was being shown to him? Did God show him in continuing his existence and in many other things—such as his living in a land of uprightness, which flowed with milk and honey, among the people who had the covenants and the law and to whom the words of God were entrusted—that he was gracious to him, that he was favorably disposed to him and filled with loving-kindness toward him in his capacity as a wicked man? Did that ungodly man receive grace? That is what Zwier teaches. He explains all these texts superficially, without paying the least attention to hundreds of scripture passages that teach the contrary.

Or is the meaning of the text that to that wicked man, living in the land of uprightness and in the midst of the people of God, God showed by everything that man received that he is gracious to the righteous and favorably disposed to his people? According to my conviction this is the meaning of the text.

There are still other reasons that Isaiah 26:10 does not fit with the common grace theory. We have called attention to these reasons more than once in the past, and it is evident from Zwier's article, in which he treats this passage, that he is well acquainted with what we wrote on this subject. But it puzzles him. He does not attempt to explain. He does not know how. Therefore, he tacitly bypasses our objections. He has considerable criticisms of his own invention, but he does not touch what we wrote against the view that this verse supports the theory of common grace. We are now thinking of the undeniable fact that this verse teaches that when grace, or favor, is shown to the wicked, he not only learns no righteousness at all, but also continues to deal crookedly and wickedly. By this manifestation of common grace sin is not restrained. Common grace is supposed to reform somewhat the unregenerate ungodly, to make a lamb out of a lion. But the grace mentioned in Isaiah 26:10 does nothing of the kind. It does not check the wrong and perverse dealings of the wicked. In fact, this truth has all the emphasis in the text. It is its main thought. Therefore, whatever the text may teach, there is no support in it for the theory of common grace as it was officially adopted in the three points by the synod of 1924.

No wonder then that Zwier does not know what to do with this undeniable fact and acts as if he never noticed this objection.

This fact was also troublesome to Hepp, as is evident from his interpretation of this verse. He tried to explain it, but his explanation shows too clearly that he does not know how to solve the difficulty. In his recent pamphlet on common grace he wrote, "Isaiah 26:10 may be paraphrased as follows: Too big a dose of common grace is not conducive to righteousness."

Hepp paraphrases the text thus to maintain the proposition that common grace is conducive to righteousness and does restrain sin in man and improve him. He evidently noticed that Isaiah 26:10 teaches the opposite. *If favor is shown to the wicked, yet he will not learn righteousness but continues to deal wrongfully in the land of uprightness.* How does Hepp try to circumvent this difficulty? He changes the term *favor* or *grace* into the phrase "too big a dose of common grace." "Yet will he not learn righteousness: in the land of uprightness will he deal unjustly" he changes into "not conducive to righteousness." He carries the following meaning into the text: a proper dose of common grace is indeed conducive to righteousness. Thus he makes the text say exactly the opposite from what it literally teaches and saves himself out of his difficulty.

However absurd such a paraphrase of the text appears to anyone not wholly blinded by a preconceived notion of common grace, Zwier tries to defend it. He admits that Hepp's paraphrase is an unhappy expression and that it could easily be wrongly interpreted, but he thinks the expression "with a little good will" can easily be understood. It is evident that when it concerns Hepp, Zwier has an abundance of good will, for he writes, "Hepp does not mean to say anything else than what Ridderbos expressed: 'When the wicked is always being spared, he hardens himself in his wickedness.' And thus understood we can readily agree with him."

However, we come back to the same point: if Zwier would thus understand Hepp's paraphrase, then the "common grace" of which Isaiah 26:10 speaks is quite different from what was officially adopted by the synod of Kalamazoo in 1924, for *this* grace certainly restrains sin not at all. Therefore we offer again our former interpretation of this text. In the main it is found in *Sin and Grace*, and later we elaborated on it in the *Standard Bearer*. With much less good will than he shows to Hepp, Zwier calls our interpretation an example of a very bad distortion of the text. But he offers no interpretation, and what must constitute an insurmountable difficulty for him, he tacitly passes by. We remain by our interpretation, which here follows.

Isaiah 26:10 is a beautiful and exalted passage of the word of God to which the notion of common grace is foreign and that teaches the opposite of what the defenders of the theory of common grace try to elicit from it. To see this we must pay attention to the context. The text is a song the church sang the day of her victory (v. 1). Her enemies have been subjected, and she has been completely delivered. Moab has been destroyed, and Babylon has been humiliated. God's people have been liberated.

When we understand this song in its final and highest significance, the people of God stand on the height of their final glorification in the day of Christ. Of the glory of the redeemed Jerusalem the church sings. It sings of the city that has foundations, a strong city that has salvation for its walls and bulwarks. Only the righteous are inhabitants of this city. They enter through the gates. They are the people who keep the truth, and the Lord keeps them in perfect peace. From the viewpoint of this city and its glory, they look back on the present. The God of this people and of this city brings down the enemies. He lays them low to the ground and brings them into the dust. God's people participate in this judgment, for they are coworkers with God. Therefore, they sing,

8. Yea, in the way of thy judgments, O Lord, have we waited for thee; the desire of our soul is to thy name, and to the remembrance of thee.
9. With my soul have I desired thee in the night; yea, with my spirit within me will I seek thee early: for when thy judgments are in the earth, the inhabitants of the world will learn righteousness. (vv. 8–9)

The redeemed church here looks back on the past. Many judgments have passed over Israel. War, pestilence, fire, sword, and famine had frequently been the lot of the people of God. But now the remnant according to the election of grace declares in its singing that they had expected and waited for the Lord and had looked for him and his coming in the way of judgments: "Yea, in the way of thy judgments, O Lord, have we waited for thee." This does not mean that they had merely hoped in him in the midst of trouble or had with certainty expected the Lord to come in the way of judgments on the world, but it emphatically means that they had looked with longing for his judgments.

Why? How could they long for the judgments of God? The answer is that in this chapter there is an expression of strong love for the Lord. This is plain from what the remnant according to the election of grace declares through the mouth of the prophet: "With my soul have I desired thee in the night; yea, with my spirit within me will I seek thee early." The remnant has zeal for the name of the Lord: "The desire of our soul is to thy name, and to the remembrance of thee." Their deepest desire is to acknowledge their God and to praise his majesty. Their prayer is "hallowed be thy name." The people of God are of God's party and as such they speak.

If the name of God is to be hallowed and glorified, his judgments are inevitable, for when God comes to judge, he empties the vials of his wrath over the ungodly. Then the inhabitants of the world will learn righteousness. This does not necessarily mean that under the pressure of God's judgments the inhabitants of the world will repent and walk in righteousness, but they certainly will learn to see, to know, and to acknowledge the righteousness of God and to behold the majesty of the Lord. When the judgments of God have been fully executed, all the inhabitants of the world will acknowledge that he is righteous, and even the damned in hell will behold and acknowledge Jehovah's majesty. That this may be realized is the strong desire of God's people. They long for the day the ungodly will be no more and the majesty of Jehovah will be universally acknowledged. Therefore, they long for God's judgments, and in the way of judgments they expect the Lord. In this connection verse 10 contrasts with verses 8–9.

Judgments must come. To show favor to the wicked is of no avail. We do not read in verse 10 that grace is actually shown to the wicked or that God is graciously disposed toward him. Literally, the text reads "Let favor be shown to the wicked, if grace is shown to him." The meaning is that this would be of absolutely no avail. If grace were shown to the wicked, it would not help. He would not learn righteousness. Judgments must come, if ever he is to acknowledge the majesty of the Lord! The text, therefore, teaches the opposite of what is implied in the theory of common grace, which teaches that if the ungodly were shown some grace, he would at least be somewhat improved and learn some righteousness. But the scriptures here teach the contrary. There is only one way the ungodly learns to know and to acknowledge the righteousness of God, and this is the way of God's judgments in which the ungodly is destroyed.

That no manifestation of favor will teach the wicked righteousness is evident. He lives in the land of uprightness. He dwells in the land of a righteous people. Thus it was among Israel. Thus it still is with the carnal seed of the church. In that land he beholds the grace of God toward his people. He perceives that God is gracious to the righteous. He hears the proclamation of this truth. He hears and beholds that God is angry with the wicked every day. In that land of uprightness he also witnesses that the righteous acknowledge the majesty of the Lord, fear him, and love him. Does all this reform the wicked? Does it change him in the least? Does it at all induce him to imitate the people of God and to practice righteousness? Not whatsoever! In the land of uprightness he deals wrongfully. Therefore let the Lord come in the way of judgments, for if favor were shown to the wicked, yet he would not learn righteousness. He practices ungodliness and iniquity in the midst of the righteous and deals unjustly in the land of justice and righteousness.

Thus it is always. The ungodly perceives that God is gracious toward his people, for he dwells in the midst of them. But his grace is not common. Grace is shown to him, so that he perceives it, but never so that he can conclude that God is gracious to him as an ungodly man. He stands outside the scope of God's grace and is well aware of it. In spite of all this, he refuses to repent, will not become righteous, and he cannot be persuaded to acknowledge the righteousness of the Lord. This he will be compelled to do only when God comes in judgments.

To the reader who is not blinded by prejudice and does not always read scripture through the strongly colored spectacles of common grace, it is plain, without a shadow of doubt, that Isaiah 26:10 teaches something quite different from Hepp's paraphrase that "too big a dose of common grace is not conducive unto righteousness."

Zwier can call our interpretation a distortion of the text and say that we carry our own idea into it. But let him prove this. If he knows of another interpretation that takes into account all the elements of the text and that can make plain that it teaches a common grace that restrains sin and improves the ungodly, let him offer it. We certainly will take notice of it.

But until now he has never even attempted to explain the text. I am convinced that he perceives the impossibility of such an interpretation. Therefore I am convinced that he will never make the attempt.

Chapter 16

The Particular Longsuffering of God

How Zwier fits the scriptures into his own preconceived notion of common grace becomes evident when he writes about the long-suffering of God (God's General Goodness, 20–22).

Although he does not hesitate to accuse us repeatedly without any proof or ground of the error of permitting our dogmatic ideas to dominate our interpretations of scripture, he himself is constantly guilty of this principal mistake. In vain one looks for interpretations of scripture in his articles. When he adduces proof from scripture for his preconceived theory of common grace, he thinks that the texts he quotes are so clear they need no explanation. When in a particular place of scripture he meets with a difficulty, a conception that is not in harmony with his notions, he closes his eyes and reasons on. He takes no account of our exegesis of the same passage of scripture, and he is evidently assured that most of his readers will never read our replies to his accusations, for impudently he attributes explanations of scripture to us that we never offered.

That I am not expressing myself too strongly I have abundantly proved in the preceding chapters. I hope to do the same regarding Zwier's explanation of the long-suffering of God.

Concerning his invention of interpretations, he writes, "But those who do not agree with this scriptural doctrine usually know how to find something, some way, to save themselves out of the difficulty these passages cause them…Just how they manage to do this with each of the texts discussed by us…I cannot say." He acknowledges that he does not know much about it. But in spite of this he writes,

> Most probably their interpretations of these texts will also be that they all apply only to the elect. When they mention the ungodly, the enemies, the wicked, the guilty, the workers of iniquity, to whom God shows his long-suffering, then in our mind we must always insert the word *elect*. For it is impossible, they say, that God can ever show the least long-suffering to one that is not elect. For him there is nothing else than hatred in God. There is no general long-suffering. This is established *a priori*, and therefore it is also impossible that these texts teach a general long-suffering of God. We met with this same argumentation before and refuted it. And, therefore, I do not deem it necessary to show in the case of each of the scriptural passages mentioned that such arbitrary interpretations of the word of God are not permissible. This is no exegesis of what the texts say, but a carrying of one's own notions into the texts. The dogmatics of these brethren dominate their exegesis.

Zwier never met with this argumentation in any of our writings. Therefore he never refuted it. Once more he becomes guilty of slander. He does not prove where we have ever used such argumentation to interpret scripture, nor did he ever prove anything like it in his preceding articles. The only difference between the article from which we quoted above and the preceding is that here he is sufficiently honest to inform his readers that he does not know how we interpret these texts. I refuse to call this brotherly.

But what method does he follow? This becomes clear when

he writes about the long-suffering of God. He begins by giving a definition of God's long-suffering.

> Also this virtue of God is a certain form of his goodness, his goodness manifested to such creatures that grievously and repeatedly sinned against him and by this became worthy of God's just punishment. Briefly expressed, God's long-suffering is his sparing goodness toward those who are worthy of punishment.

He *starts* by giving a definition of God's long-suffering. Where did he derive his definition? It certainly is not the scriptures, for he refers to scripture much later not for the purpose of formulating a definition of long-suffering, but simply to carry his established definition into the texts. Did Zwier deduce his definition from the meaning of *long-suffering*? Also this cannot be true, for what he expresses in the definition is certainly not implied in the word in the Hebrew and Greek, or in the Dutch language in which he writes. It is possible that he found his definition in some dogmatic work. In that case he certainly causes dogmatics to dominate his exegesis. It is also possible that he arbitrarily formulated a definition of his own. In that case he subjects the word of God to his philosophy.

This is exactly what an exegete may not do. If it is our intention to formulate a scriptural definition of any concept, we begin by investigating scripture, compare the several passages in scripture where the concept we would define occurs, exegete them, and then finally base our definition on the exegesis of these passages. If Zwier would investigate our writings before he informs others about our teachings, he would have to admit that we have always followed this scriptural method.

Still more, before he even refers to scripture, he establishes that there is a general and particular long-suffering of God. The concept long-suffering he distinguishes as "general" and "particular."

The Particular Longsuffering of God

Also with regard to this virtue of God we must on the basis of scripture distinguish between a manifestation of it in a narrower and in a wider scope. There is a particular long-suffering that God shows to his elect unto eternal life, and there is a general long-suffering that he shows to the nonelect.

Between these two there is not a gradual difference but an essential difference.

That is, the matter is not thus, that God manifests very much long-suffering to the elect and but a little of the same long-suffering to the others. This would be a difference of degree, a question of more or less. But this is not the case with God's long-suffering. There is an essential difference between his long-suffering he shows to the elect and his long-suffering he shows to the nonelect.

In both cases God's long-suffering is his sparing goodness toward those who are worthy of punishment. Because of this scripture can use the same word for both. But the essential difference between both becomes immediately evident when we say that God's long-suffering to his elect is always accompanied with complete pardon, while his long-suffering to the nonelect does not imply more than a *postponement* of punishment.

I am inclined to suspect that Zwier looked for words when he wrote that last paragraph. His intention was to point out the *essential* difference between particular and general long-suffering. One would expect that to do that he would clearly and definitely define what particular long-suffering is and what general long-suffering is. How otherwise can an *essential* difference be indicated? Yet he does not do this. He writes, "God's long-suffering to his elect is always accompanied with complete pardon, while his long-suffering to the nonelect does not imply more than a *postponement* of punishment."

Why does Zwier express himself thus? Why does he try to impress his readers that he points out an *essential* difference, while it is evident that he does not do this? You cannot indicate an essential difference between two concepts by saying that one concept is *accompanied* by something that the other concept is not. Why did Zwier not write that particular long-suffering *is* acquittal from punishment and that general long-suffering *is* postponement of punishment? I suspect that he understood that then he would have no particular long-suffering left, for if long-suffering is God's goodness to those who are worthy of punishment, long-suffering certainly ceases where one is completely acquitted. Hence he uses the expression "is always accompanied."

Once more we ask, why does Zwier so vaguely write "is always accompanied"? What is the relation between long-suffering and acquittal from punishment? There certainly must be an essential relation between those two according to Zwier's conception. Is particular long-suffering based on acquittal from punishment? Why then did Zwier not write that? I surmise that he realized that if he would express himself so definitely regarding particular long-suffering, he would be compelled to do the same with general long-suffering. Then he would come face to face with the troublesome question, what is the basis for the postponement of punishment? He proceeds from the assumption that there is goodness, loving-kindness, a favorable disposition in God concerning the reprobate ungodly. An *essential* difference between his particular and his general long-suffering cannot be said to exist, and therefore I suppose that Zwier intentionally expresses himself so ambiguously. He *cannot* say, "Particular long-suffering *is*..., and general long-suffering *is*..." If he would do that, he would have to say that particular long-suffering *is* sparing goodness, mercy, and favor of God toward those who are worthy of punishment, and general long-suffering *is* sparing goodness, mercy, and favor of God toward those who are worthy of punishment. Thus he taught his readers in the beginning: "In both cases God's long-suffering is his sparing goodness toward those who are worthy of punishment."

The Particular Longsuffering of God

Thus Zwier knows of no *essential* difference between the two. When he nevertheless speaks of such an essential difference, he avoids the difficulty by the words "is always accompanied." If one does watch (and Zwier depends on it that most of his readers fail to do this), you are very neatly being deceived.

All this he established before he refers to scripture. Then he writes, "This will become still more evident to us when we investigate the few texts that speak of the long-suffering of God." These few texts now must serve to make still more evident what he has established beforehand.

Zwier refers first to Luke 18:7. According to his notion this text elucidates the particular long-suffering of God.

> In the parable of the unjust judge Jesus makes the following application: "And shall not God avenge his own elect, which cry day and night unto him, though he bear long with them [his long-suffering over them]?" This declaration needs no interpretation.

"This declaration needs no interpretation." This is all Zwier offers! We have gradually become accustomed to the following statements in his writings: The texts are so plain they need no explanation. The texts speak for themselves. A child can understand them. One with even a quarter of an ounce of understanding can comprehend them. Zwier has declared these statements repeatedly in preceding articles, and now he writes again, "This declaration needs no interpretation." One cannot really say that he permits dogmatics to dominate his exegesis because exegesis is absent.

If Zwier's definition of long-suffering is inserted into this passage instead of the words "bear long," the result is: "Shall not God avenge his own elect, which cry day and night unto him, although in his sparing goodness he bears with them, worthy of punishment though they may be?" The definition does not fit. It changes the meaning of the text into exactly the opposite from what the Lord meant to say, as is evident from the context. Then the text means that although God still spares his elect in his long-suffering, he will presently punish them in his justice. But Jesus says, "Shall not God avenge his own elect upon their enemies, although he postpones the urge of his love to deliver them?" Certainly there is no mention in Luke 18:7 of a "sparing goodness of God toward those who are worthy of punishment."

According to the parable God's people are treated unjustly and are oppressed in the world. From the depth of their oppression they cry to God for justice, for him to avenge them of their adversaries. The parable has the definite purpose of teaching God's people to pray always for this justice of God and for revenge upon their enemies. It seems that God does not hear their prayers. The time is long. Deliverance is postponed. God's people groan and cry for justice, but the Lord does not answer. How to explain this? God is long-suffering over them! What does this mean? Sparing goodness toward the guilty? Nothing of the kind! The elect are not viewed here as objects of wrath worthy of punishment, but as the oppressed who suffer injustice, as objects of God's eternal love whom he longs to deliver. Longsuffering therefore is here no stretched-out wrath, but love that postpones the final deliverance of its objects because the time of final deliverance and justification of the elect has not yet come.

This interpretation is not new. Repeatedly we have offered it since 1923.

It ought to be evident that Zwier's preestablished definition of the long-suffering of God does not fit this passage. And he cannot excuse himself by saying that the text needs no interpretation. He certainly will have to change his dogmatics on this point in the light of the proper interpretation of this text.

A second text to which Zwier refers to prove God's particular "sparing goodness toward those who are worthy of punishment" is 1 Timothy 1:15–16.

> The apostle Paul, looking back at the time he had been a slanderer, a persecutor, and an oppressor of the church

declares that he obtained mercy so that in him first Jesus might show forth all long-suffering for a pattern to those who would hereafter believe on him to life everlasting. Also this declaration is sufficiently clear without further interpretation.

Notice that the foundation of Zwier's exegesis is that scripture passages are sufficiently clear without interpretation.

If Zwier's definition of long-suffering is inserted into the text it reads as follows: "This is a faithful saying, and worthy of all acceptation, that Christ Jesus came into the world to save sinners; of whom I am chief. Howbeit for this cause I obtained mercy, that in me first Jesus Christ might shew forth all his sparing goodness toward those who are worthy of punishment, for a pattern to those who would hereafter believe on him to life everlasting."

Also with respect to this text Zwier's definition of the long-suffering of God fails to fit. There is no mention or any thought of a sparing goodness toward the guilty in the verse. "Longsuffering" in the text means unchangeable, all-bearing Redeemer's love, that became manifest when Paul was drawn by that love. If long-suffering here means sparing goodness, it could have been manifested much more effectively by not converting Paul, by allowing him to continue his persecution and oppression of the church and disciples of Christ, and then by sparing him. But that long-suffering was revealed by showing mercy to Paul. Christ drew him with cords of love to manifest his long-suffering. When the text is thus interpreted, long-suffering means an unchangeable and a redeeming love that cannot be quenched. This is probably the correct interpretation, since Paul repeatedly designated himself as the chief of sinners.

We admit that another interpretation is possible. It would be in agreement with other passages in Holy Writ and with a common meaning of long-suffering, to interpret the text as "I have obtained mercy, in order that in the cause of Christ I should suffer much, and thus the long-suffering of Jesus Christ might become manifest in my suffering as an example to those who would believe in him." This would agree with Acts 9:15–16: "But the Lord said unto him, Go thy way: for he is a chosen vessel unto me, to bear my name before the Gentiles, and kings, and the children of Israel: for I will shew him how great things he must suffer for my name's sake."

Whatever interpretation you prefer, Zwier's definition of God's long-suffering as his "sparing goodness toward those who are worthy of punishment" certainly does not fit 1 Timothy 1:16.

Zwier has one more text to prove the sparing goodness of God toward the elect. It is 2 Peter 3:9.

> The apostle Peter, treating of the coming of the Lord, explains that his coming is being postponed for the elect's sake: "The Lord is not slack concerning his promise, as some men count slackness; but is longsuffering to us-ward, not willing that any should perish but that all should come to repentance." Also here, as is plain from the context, the reference is to God's long-suffering over his church, which is gathered in this dispensation and of which not one person may be lost. The apostle in his admonition in verse 15 refers again to God's long-suffering: "account that the longsuffering of our Lord is salvation.

Also here Zwier offers no interpretation, but only the remark that it is plain that the reference is to God's long-suffering toward his church. We fully agree with him, but he should have shown that this passage supports his definition of God's long-suffering. We do not agree with Zwier when he asserts that the apostle teaches that the coming of the Lord is postponed for the elects' sake. The text emphatically teaches that God is not slack concerning his promise. Therefore, he does not postpone the coming of the Lord, although some think he does. Instead of thinking that the Lord is slack, they must understand that the Lord is long-suffering toward them. The meaning is therefore that God, by virtue of his great love for his people, would gladly deliver and glorify them at once, but he stretches out his love until all the elect will have been gathered.

This text has the same idea as the parable of the unjust judge. God's people must suffer much, and in their suffering they long for the coming of the Lord. They pray for Christ to come quickly. When that prayer is not heard immediately, they complain that God is slack concerning his promise. But even as in the parable of the unjust judge, so here the church is assured that God will avenge them quickly, that he is not slack concerning his promise, although he is long-suffering toward his people.

But when Zwier's definition is inserted for the word "longsuffering," the text makes no sense, for it reads: "The Lord is not slack concerning his promise, as some men count slackness; but he assumes an attitude of sparing goodness toward us, his guilty church, worthy of punishment, not willing that any should perish, but that all should come to repentance." Thus the text would make no sense.

The church is not viewed as guilty and as the object of God's just wrath, but as the object of the love of God and as suffering under oppression in the world. God does not say to this church, "I really ought to punish you because of your sins, but I will temporarily spare you." But he says to her, "I will deliver you as soon as possible in my love, and I am not slack concerning that promise, but you must show a little patience until the time is ripe for your final redemption."

The same thought is expressed in James 5:7: "Be patient therefore, brethren, unto the coming of the Lord. Behold, the husbandman waiteth for the precious fruit of the earth, and hath long patience for it, until he receive the early and latter rain." I do not have to point out how the definition of Zwier would not fit in this passage. Everyone can see that for himself.

It is evident therefore that Zwier did not give the scriptural idea of long-suffering when he defined it as "sparing goodness toward those who are worthy of punishment." He will certainly have to alter his dogmatics.

Chapter 17

The General Longsuffering of God

In the previous chapter I demonstrated that Zwier first gives a definition of the long-suffering of God. Thereupon he establishes that God's long-suffering is particular and general. Finally he attempts to support with scripture the dogmatic propositions that he has *a priori* established.

It is evident that Zwier's definition of the long-suffering of God is not supported by those passages of scripture we have discussed and in which he thought he could find his notion of God's particular long-suffering.

Let us now examine the texts that in Zwier's opinion corroborate his notion of the general long-suffering of God, that is, the doctrine that God in his loving kindness spares the ungodly. He refers first to Romans 2:4, which I discussed in chapters 7 and 14. It is sufficient to refer the reader to those chapters.

A second text in which Zwier finds the general long-suffering of God is 1 Peter 3:19–20. "By which [the Spirit] also he [Christ] went and preached unto the spirit's in prison; which sometime were disobedient, when once the longsuffering of God waited in the days of Noah, while the ark was a preparing, wherein few, that is, eight souls were saved by water." In explaining this text he writes, "We need not touch on the difficulties connected with the exegesis, because they have nothing to do with the point in question." This is regrettable. In reality it is never true that the difficulties of a text have nothing to do with a certain point in question. At least one cannot establish this until he has attempted to explain those difficulties. When such an attempt is made, frequently the result is that new light is shed on the point in question. But Zwier passes by those difficulties. He adopts the generally accepted Reformed interpretation "that the spirits in prison are the ungodly contemporaries of Noah to whom Christ preached not after his resurrection, as is the Roman Catholic and Lutheran view, but in the days before the flood through his prophet Noah, the preacher of righteousness. They are called 'spirits in prison' because they are preserved in the place of darkness unto the judgment of the great day." Adopting this interpretation, Zwier teaches concerning the long-suffering of God that it was shown "to the ungodly contemporaries of Noah for a hundred and twenty years while the ark was being prepared. The punishment was long postponed. Opportunity was given them to repent." Then he concludes, "Clearly it is also evident here that the long-suffering of God is shown to the ungodly."

Against Zwier's interpretation, which he adopts without any investigation of the text, there are insurmountable objections. His interpretation is the result of an attempt to escape the Romish and Lutheran explanations of the text rather than of independent exegesis. The Roman Catholic interpretation is that after his death Christ entered the portals of hell and delivered the old dispensational believers and took them to paradise. The Lutheran interpretation is that Christ literally descended into hell, both in his Godhead and his humanity, announced his victory there, and deprived the devil of his power. Against these interpretations Reformed commentators teach that the preaching of Christ in the Spirit refers to the Savior's preaching to the ungodly world during the days of Noah.

Serious objections can be raised against the last interpretation.

It cannot be denied that the context of the passage compels us to think of something that took place after the suffering and glorification of Christ, for in verse 18 we read, "Christ also hath once suffered for sins, the just for the unjust, that he might bring us to God, being put to death in the flesh, but quickened by the Spirit." Then we read in verse 19, "by which also he went and preached unto the spirits in prison." "By which" refers to the Spirit of Christ's resurrection and glorification, and it is incorrect to say that the apostle suddenly goes back in his mind hundreds of years in order to teach that the resurrected and glorified Christ preached through Noah to the ungodly world of his day. This interpretation is too obviously false and does not fit the context. According to the context, the preaching must be conceived as taking place after the Savior's suffering and glorification.

The text also teaches this. We read that Jesus preached to the spirits that "are" in prison. This is very clear in the original, which translated literally is "to the [being] in prison spirits." Besides, we read that those spirits were disobedient "formerly" or "sometime." "Sometime" refers to a time that preceded not only their being in prison, but also the preaching. If the apostle had meant to say that Christ had *formerly* preached to the spirits that are now in prison, how easily he could have expressed that by the pluperfect instead of the aorist or by placing "sometime" immediately before or after "preached." In that case the text would read, "By which also he formerly [sometime] had gone and had preached to the spirits, who at the time of Noah were disobedient and are now in prison." But the text says that the preaching took place not formerly and to living men who are now in prison, but to spirits in prison who formerly were disobedient.

The text teaches that the Savior, through the Spirit he received after his glorification (Acts 2:33), went to preach to the spirits who are preserved in prison unto the day of judgment. The text does not teach that Jesus descended personally and literally into hell.

The General Longsuffering of God

The preaching was through the Spirit, through whom he also condemns the world. Nor does the text teach that he preached the *gospel* to those spirits. This is not implied in the word "preached." The context shows that by this preaching Jesus witnessed of his glorification and victory that he had obtained for himself and his people. This is also the reason the text mentions the spirits who were disobedient at the time of Noah. They were types of the ungodly of the latter days and represented the entire ungodly world. That they raged terribly against the church of those days can easily be shown from scripture. This is also the underlying thought of the text, as is evident from the context. In that context the apostle writes about the suffering believers have to endure from the wicked world, and he encourages them to suffer with a good conscience for well-doing and not as evil-doers. Christ also suffered for doing well, the just for the unjust. He also gained the victory and received honor and glory. He announced that to the ungodly world, including those who sometimes persecuted him and his people at the time of Noah. Christ witnessed that by the Spirit of his glorification.

In the light of all this I am convinced that Zwier erroneously interprets the text. Without any proof he takes for granted that the long-suffering of God refers to the goodness of God whereby he spared for a hundred and twenty years the ungodly world at the time of Noah. The text does not say that God was long-suffering over the disobedient at the time of Noah, but declares that the long-suffering of God waits. This word makes us think of the attitude of God's suffering and oppressed people during Noah's days. In 2 Peter 3:9 the apostle in a similar connection speaks of God's "longsuffering to us-ward," that is, toward the church. The context also speaks of God's long-suffering toward his people who must suffer much from the world. Therefore the long-suffering of God mentioned in 1 Peter 3:20 refers to the attitude of waiting love that God revealed before the flood to his church, which had to suffer much from the spirits that are now in prison. The church looked for deliverance. But the long-suffering of God waited: the deliverance did not come as quickly as the people of God expected.

What Zwier remarks about Nahum 1:2–3 is rather poor.

> The book of the vision of Nahum the Elkoshite contains a proclamation of the judgment of God over the ungodly city of Nineveh and commences as follows: "God is jealous, and the LORD revengeth; the LORD revengeth, and is furious; the LORD will take vengeance on his adversaries, and he reserveth wrath for his enemies. The LORD is slow to anger [long-suffering], and great in power, and will not at all acquit the wicked."[For "slow to anger" the Dutch has *lankmoedigheid* (long-suffering).]
>
> It is absolutely impossible to understand "slow to anger" in this text as referring to the people of God. Nahum 1 does not speak of God's people until verse 7: "The LORD is good, a stronghold in the day of trouble; and he knoweth them that trust in him." Read the first six verses, and it will be clear that the reference throughout is to the ungodly, to God's adversaries, his enemies, the guilty, who are worthy of God's wrath. The entire context, therefore, shows that the expression "the LORD is slow to anger" refers to the ungodly. (God's General Goodness, 21)

Zwier's exegesis is so superficial that it is unworthy of the name. All he really proves is that the Dutch word for long-suffering is used to denote God's attitude toward the ungodly. Who would not immediately grant him that point? Zwier apparently relies too strongly on his presupposition that wherever "long-suffering" occurs in scripture we apply it to the elect. He has the notion that we also follow this method with the text in Nahum, so that we explain the "adversaries," "guilty," and the others as referring to the elect. With this preconceived notion he imagines that he scores a

The General Longsuffering of God

victory when he says that the entire context proves that the expression "the Lord is slow to anger" refers to the ungodly.

Certainly, Zwier saw this correctly, but if exegetical ability is measured by quarters of an ounce, as seems to be his opinion, we can say that it did not require a quarter of an ounce of exegetical acumen to discover this truth. Sad to say, however, that this proves nothing with regard to the point in question, for he writes about the general goodness of God, and long-suffering, according to him, is sparing goodness toward the guilty. The text in Nahum must serve him to prove that there is a *general* long-suffering of God, that is, a long-suffering toward the just and the unjust. What remains of Zwier's alleged proof in this text from Nahum when you consider what he tries to prove by it? How is it possible to find the theory of common grace, common loving-kindness, or common long-suffering in this passage?

Even the Dutch text should have been sufficient warning to Zwier that his pet theory is not corroborated by it. It should be evident to anyone, even to Zwier, that there is no mention in the text of general long-suffering, but of a very limited and particular long-suffering that refers only to the ungodly. We admit without reservation that it is clear that the expression "the Lord is slow to anger" refers only to the ungodly. I even want to emphasize this and insist that it refers only to the wicked. But certainly, long-suffering that is only for the ungodly cannot be called general or common.

In addition, the whole text should have been sufficient warning to Zwier that it cannot be quoted as a proof for the theory of God's sparing goodness toward the ungodly. Reading the text, he should immediately have said to himself, "Whatever may be the significance of the Dutch word in this passage, it certainly does not have the meaning of sparing goodness. The entire passage speaks of vengeance, of great anger, of a reserving of wrath for the enemies of God, of a refusal to acquit the wicked. Therefore it is impossible not only that the expression "the Lord is long-suffering" could be applied to God's people, but also that it could have the significance of a sparing goodness of God."

When Zwier understood this, he should have asked himself, "What is the significance of the word 'longsuffering' in Nahum 1:3?" If the Hebrew is somewhat obnoxious to him, he might have looked up the verse in his English Bible. The English text might have helped him, for it translates the Hebrew as "slow to anger." This is something quite different from sparing goodness, which is always goodness. But slowness to anger is anger and wrath. Repressed anger, which is reserved and accompanied by great wrath, is quite different from sparing goodness, favor, loving-kindness, or whatever term you prefer. He might have recalled that the word "long-suffering," just as the Greek word *makrothumia*, is a neutral word that expresses that a certain feeling, emotion, or disposition is long. But what kind of emotion or disposition is long the word does not express. This emotion may be the urge of love that is long repressed, but it can be the feeling of wrath that is long restrained. If Zwier had taken his exegesis more seriously and at least made a little study of the Hebrew text, instead of being deceived by the sound of a Dutch word, he would have discovered that "long-suffering" in this passage is a translation of two Hebrew words: *erek appajim*. The first word means "long" or "length," and the second word signifies "wrath" (derived from *aph*, breath). The Lord therefore is long of wrath. He is very angry with the ungodly and will certainly destroy them, but he stretches out his wrath until the time is ripe for the ultimate destruction of the wicked.

After Zwier had discovered this and made a little study of other scriptural passages that use the same word, and if he had been honest for the truth's sake, he would have concluded on the basis of scripture that the distinction I have always made between forbearance and long-suffering is right, although the Dutch and English Bibles do not always maintain this distinction. Zwier certainly would have acknowledged that Nahum does not speak of any goodness of God at all, sparing or otherwise. I certainly hope that in the future Zwier will not offer exegesis that is based on the sound of a Dutch word.

He writes, "With a view to these scriptural passages, it is a riddle to me how the brethren who stumbled in 1924 dared to maintain that we may not speak of a general long-suffering of God. It transcends my comprehension."

I gladly believe him. But the trouble was certainly with Zwier's comprehension, not with the "stumbled brethren" having no ground for their contentions.

Perhaps the above will shed light on another riddle of which Zwier speaks. He thinks it is a great riddle that I can interpret Romans 9:22 as I do.

Nevertheless, I will try to shed a little more light on the familiar text: "What if God, willing to shew his wrath, and to make his power known, endured with much longsuffering the vessels of wrath fitted unto destruction." My interpretation was that God endured the vessels of wrath with much long-suffering over the vessels of mercy.

My grounds for this interpretation are as follows:

First, in the New Testament long-suffering usually signifies restrained love toward the church as she must suffer in the world and is oppressed by that world.

Second, both forbearance and long-suffering occur in the text, but the vessels of wrath are the direct objects of forbearance, while long-suffering is presented as accompanying this forbearance.

Third, the context mentions Pharaoh as the representative of the vessels of wrath. Israel in Egypt suffered much and was sorely oppressed through Pharaoh's ungodliness. Thus it is always in the world. The wicked always set themselves against the righteous; the wicked hate and persecute the righteous.

Fourth, when God does not immediately destroy the vessels of wrath and forbears them, that is, he is long of wrath and represses his anger until the judgment day, the result is that the children of God must suffer and be persecuted. For this reason God's forbearance toward the vessels of wrath is always accompanied by long-suffering toward his people.

Fifth, I arrived at this meaning of the text: What if God, willing to show his wrath and to make his power known, endured the vessels of wrath fitted unto destruction with much long-suffering over his people, who must suffer much on account of the vessels of wrath.

Zwier makes much ado about my interpretation. For years it was a riddle to him how we could maintain such an explanation. It is beyond him. He finds it to be "the most flagrant example of arbitrary exegesis and wanton carrying into the text one's notions." In many years he has not seen the like. He imagines that I insert the words "toward his people" into this passage to maintain that God can never be long-suffering over the ungodly.

Much ado about nothing!

Even though on the above-mentioned grounds I prefer my interpretation of the text, I gladly grant Zwier that the other interpretation, which is that the expression "endured with much long-suffering" refers to the vessels of wrath, can very well be defended on exegetical grounds. I do not attach as much significance to my interpretation as Zwier thinks. It is certainly not true that I offered my interpretation to avoid the conception that God's long-suffering is ever toward the ungodly. I had no need of this, for even if we accept that long-suffering and forbearance must be explained as referring to the vessels of wrath, we thereby have not in the least admitted that the text supports the notion of a general goodness of God manifested as long-suffering. In that case this passage uses long-suffering to denote an attitude of God only toward the ungodly.

If one would find support for the notion of a general goodness of God in the text, he certainly would have to do more than merely show that long-suffering is used here with application to the vessels of wrath. He would have to prove that the word in this connection means "sparing goodness toward the guilty." Zwier proceeded from a dogmatic definition of long-suffering without first consulting scripture.

But I have proved that the definition of long-suffering as "sparing goodness toward the guilty" cannot be derived from the term itself. I have also shown that this definition fits nowhere in the texts that Zwier quoted to support his contention. If Romans 9:22 can support his idea, he will still have to prove that. All he proves is that according to his interpretation, long-suffering refers to the vessels of wrath. Then he writes, "Therefore, we have here a clear proof that besides the particular long-suffering of God shown only to the elect to eternal life, there is also a certain general long-suffering of God that he manifests to the nonelect in the postponement of their punishment and in an opportunity to repent."

His conclusion does not follow from his premise, and it certainly does not harmonize with the text. Zwier is again guilty of distorting the text to make it teach the exact opposite of what it actually signifies. This is especially clear when the text is viewed in connection with the entire chapter.

If we adopt the interpretation that applies long-suffering to the vessels of wrath, the text still does not teach a general long-suffering. The text speaks of a particular long-suffering toward the reprobate.

According to Zwier we must read the text as follows: "What if God, willing to shew his sparing goodness to the ungodly and to give them time to repent, endured with much longsuffering the vessels of wrath fitted unto destruction." This is impossible. Zwier's definition of long-suffering does not fit in this text, which teaches that the vessels of wrath were fitted unto destruction. Of God's granting an opportunity to repent there is certainly no mention. The text also teaches that God endures the vessels of wrath with much long-suffering to show his wrath and make his power known. Of a general goodness the text does not speak at all. Therefore Zwier will have to admit that this text does not support his pet theory of common grace. Whatever interpretation of the text you prefer, it certainly does not mention a sparing goodness of God toward the guilty.

Zwier has one more text to prove his conception of a general long-suffering. He points to the parable of the unmerciful servant and says that long-suffering was shown to the unmerciful servant, and he was proven to be a wicked man who was surrendered to eternal torture.

This interpretation of the parable cannot be maintained for a moment. The long-suffering, or mercy, that the Lord of the parable shows to his servant is forgiving all his debt.

According to Zwier only particular long-suffering is accompanied by remission of punishment. We have not forgotten this. When he makes the long-suffering in the parable general, we hold him to his word and say, "Just a moment, Zwier. This will not do!"

Zwier's presentation that the unmerciful servant in the parable is an ungodly man, a person without grace, cannot be maintained because it leads to the conclusion that God first forgives the sins of the nonelect and then repents and imputes their sins to them. This is impossible.

Zwier admits all this. He writes, "We understand that this cannot be true."

For this reason he simply passes by this main element in the parable and does not mention the fact that the lord forgave his servant all his debt. Zwier simply acts as if this element were not in the parable or what is worse, he denies it. This too is not permissible, for if we do not take into account the element of the lord's forgiving the servant's debt, the whole parable loses its significance.

For this reason the servant of the parable certainly must represent someone other than a reprobate wicked who is consigned to eternal desolation. Nor does the text say this, for it says, "His lord was wroth, and delivered him to the tormentors till he should pay all that was due unto him" (Matt. 18:34). If we read the context and do not allow dogmatic prejudices to stand in the way of a correct understanding of the parable, it is clear that the servant in the parable is a child of God, who is unwilling to reconcile and forgive his brother and is delivered to the tormentors for a time. This means that as long as he refuses to reconcile and to forgive, he will not taste the forgiving grace of God.

This interpretation agrees with the context. Jesus spoke this parable to his disciples, more particularly to Peter. Hence we may say that he spoke it to his elect people. Peter's opinion was that the obligation to forgive one another must have limits. Jesus said to him, "No, Peter, not seven times, but seventy times seven times you must forgive your brother. There is never an end to this obligation in the kingdom of God. The kingdom of God may be likened to this king and his dealings with an unmerciful servant. Therefore, I say to you, Peter, and to you, my disciples, my people: so likewise shall my heavenly Father do also unto you, if you from your hearts forgive not everyone his brother his trespasses."

Thus it is clear that Zwier's interpretation is untenable.

The strong desire to find support for his theory of a general long-suffering of God makes it impossible for him to understand the parable.

Chapter 18

Conclusion

In the light of scripture, I have carefully reviewed Zwier's series of articles on God's general goodness.

It became evident that all twenty-eight articles on this subject contain nothing else than a defense of the first of the three points adopted by the Kalamazoo synod in 1924. He commenced by pointing out that the synod of 1924 exhorted the leaders of the Christian Reformed Church to study and to develop further the doctrine of common grace, and he called it inexcusable neglect that that had not been done. But in his articles he certainly made no attempt to comply with that exhortation. After writing a few introductory articles, it soon became clear that he had no other intention than to defend the first point of common grace. He made no serious attempt in the entire series of articles to develop a certain line or to offer a carefully defined conception of common grace.

It also became clear that his system of doctrine is a hopeless dualism that is necessary to defend the first point and to maintain the appearance that he also subscribed to the Reformed truth of particular grace. Doctrinally there are two Zwiers who cannot be united into one. Zwier calls this incongruous and contradictory element in his conception a mystery. He imagines that he finds the same contradiction in the scriptures and maintains that simple

Conclusion

faith readily accepts the most exclusive contradictions. In my criticism of Zwier's conception I merely took account of one Zwier—the one of common grace.

I also proved time and again with quotations from his articles that Zwier does not hesitate to misrepresent us to his readers and to attribute teachings to us that have never been ours. This is especially true of his presentation of my method of interpreting scripture. I have conclusively shown that in reality he never offers any exegesis worthy of the name of those scriptural passages to which he appeals in support of his theory. While one needs little exegetical ability to see that my interpretations of texts are distortions of scripture, the texts to which he appeals are usually so self-evident that they need no interpretation.

However, I did not base my view on a few passages of scripture, but appealed to the current teaching of the Bible and in the light of it explained some individual texts.

This chapter is my conclusion.

According to the scheme I originally made, I inserted a few other matters I intended to discuss. There is, for example, the appeal of Zwier to the prayer of Jonah (Jonah 4:2) and to Jude 1:4 concerning the reprobate who change the grace of God into lasciviousness. Zwier does not know very well what value he must attach to the "grumbling" Jonah (of whom I have a higher opinion than Zwier), and his interpretation of Jude 1:4 is too puerile to be worthy of my attention. Besides, I have discussed all the main points of Zwier's articles. If I have overlooked anything he considers to be important, I hope he will be kind enough to call my attention to it. Finally, this series has become sufficiently long and should now be finished, especially since the intention of the Reformed Free Publishing Association is to publish it in the Dutch and English languages, in order to reach the readers for whom Zwier wrote his articles.

Before I close, however, I must call attention to a few matters.

The first matter concerns the way Zwier attempts to convince his readers that he and Greydanus of Kampen perfectly agree with each other. Our readers may know that Greydanus recently developed in a series of questions a few thoughts concerning common grace. Zwier writes that we had great expectations of Greydanus' speech, greeted it with high acclaim, and imagined that finally we had support in the Netherlands for our ideas. However, Zwier claims that we cling to a straw, but he is not offended. He writes, "There is and remains a profound difference between their ideas and those of the brethren in the Netherlands."

We will pay no more attention to these big words. We can afford to let the truth quietly do its work. The facts will undoubtedly compel Zwier to swallow his high-sounding phrases. Concerning this there can be little doubt. We can afford quietly to wait what the future will bring. There is one important thing in our favor: we have nothing to conceal. We have no need of camouflage to give the brethren in the Netherlands a good impression of our conception and of our history. The more our case appears in its true light, the more we are bound to gain and the darker becomes the page the Christian Reformed Church wrote in its historic record in 1924. We can therefore be at peace.

Zwier expresses the opinion that we distorted matters when we wrote that for the very views that Greydanus developed in question form, we were expelled from the Christian Reformed Church. But I would like to ask him: was it not most recently proven that the Christian Reformed Church would be inclined also to expel men such as Schilder and Greydanus? Was not the attempt made to frustrate Schilder's visit to our country? And when that attempt failed, did they not try to boycott him? How was he treated here in the Christian Reformed Jerusalem, where the "big four" rule? These attempts were inspired only by the uncertainty concerning Schilder's convictions concerning common grace. When the leaders of the Christian Reformed Church are so eager to keep an esteemed guest out of our country, would they not much rather cast him out of their churches?

Conclusion

Zwier expresses the opinion that we do him an injustice when we say that he changes his views somewhat in order to leave the impression that he is in perfect agreement with Greydanus. According to Zwier there is no doubt about this. But I will prove with facts that Zwier does "heave to" and misrepresent matters on three points: first, regarding what Greydanus calls a mystery; second, regarding Greydanus' statement that one must remain on the surface of things in order to speak of common grace; third, regarding Greydanus' declared opinion that we are not yet prepared to establish an ecclesiastical dogma of common grace.

First, concerning the mystery, I quote from Zwier's articles what Greydanus wrote about this.

> In all this man is undoubtedly the guilty party. No lost person will be able to accuse God in the place of desolation that he unjustly cast him into destruction. Far be God from wickedness and the Almighty from unrighteousness. But this does not alter or deny the fact that God from eternity has known, willed, and determined their eternal destination—the sad and final result of their use of the goods God bestowed on them, of their existence, of their talents, of their power, and of their knowledge of the gospel. God's intention was never to work their eternal salvation through all these means. Here we face a divine mystery that we cannot solve.

What is the divine mystery that Greydanus cannot solve? Is it expressed in the question, how can God be gracious in time to those whom he has reprobated from eternity? No. The mystery is, how can God determine and will the final outcome of the life and walk of the ungodly, and yet they are the responsible and guilty parties?

But how does Zwier represent him?

> Dr. Greydanus, and we with him, accepts what the scriptures teach in Psalm 73:18, Psalm 92:7–8, Proverbs 16:4, and Exodus 9:16. But Greydanus, and we with him, also

accepts what the Bible teaches in Romans 11:11, Lamentations 3:33, Ezekiel 18:23, and Ezekiel 33:11. Greydanus, and we with him, acknowledges that these scriptural declarations confront us with a divine mystery, and the solution is withheld from us. Before this divine mystery we bow reverently without attempting to solve it.

Here Zwier misrepresents matters. His mystery is radically different from that of Greydanus, and he certainly must know this. The mystery with Greydanus is that God sovereignly does all his good pleasure, yet man is responsible. This is not an absurdity. The two parts of this declaration do not contradict each other. But Zwier's mystery is that God gives to the ungodly reprobate the things of this present time unto their damnation (Ps. 73, Ps. 92, and many other passages), and he gives him those same things in his grace. This certainly is an absurdity. It is not a mystery at all. It is nonsense. Zwier is simply playing on words. A child can see this, and he will have to admit it.

Second, I quote Greydanus from Zwier's articles regarding Greydanus' statement that one must remain on the surface of things in order to maintain the doctrine of common grace.

> One who is satisfied with the superficial—our unmerited and forfeited rights, no obligation on God's part, the visible and temporal—may soon have his mind made up on the matter of common grace. But one who looks into eternity and takes into account what God has revealed concerning his counsel, beholds mysteries and is not so ready with his answer.

Does Greydanus intend us to be satisfied with the superficial and continue to speak of common grace? The reader will grant immediately that his words signify the opposite. One who is satisfied with the superficial is soon ready to answer and has no difficulty making up his mind regarding common grace. But one who

Conclusion

takes into account the revelation of God's eternal good pleasure, as every Reformed man should do, does not have an easy and ready answer. Greydanus condemns the attitude that would remain on the surface of things.

What does Zwier write about this?

> When Greydanus declares with respect to all the good God bestows on the nonelect, we cannot speak of grace when we consider the eternal results caused by their abuse of God's good gifts, so that it had been better for those who received those gifts if they had not been born. Besides, remember what scripture teaches concerning the unchangeable counsel of God by which this terrible final outcome is determined from eternity. Then every Reformed man will also agree with him on this point. When we speak of general or common grace, it is indeed true that we remain on the surface of things and consider only visible and temporal things. We do not inquire regarding the ground of things. This is permissible because scripture gives the example. (God's General Goodness, 26)

Zwier "heaves to" and misrepresents matters. Greydanus taught that if we are satisfied with only the superficial, we can quickly be ready to speak of common grace, but a Reformed man may not be satisfied with the surface of things. Zwier pretends that he perfectly agrees with him, but conveniently overlooks the last part of Greydanus' statement. Zwier claims that he is satisfied with the superficial, and this is permissible because it is scriptural. Zwier is well aware, in spite of what writes, that on this point he does not at all agree with Greydanus.

Finally, I call attention to Greydanus' opinion that the church is not ready to formulate ecclesiastical dogmas concerning common grace. I quote Zwier:

> The speaker [Greydanus] began by saying that the problem of general, or common, grace belongs to the points

that need more profound investigation and wider discussion before there can be a sufficiently clear insight of faith to formulate ecclesiastical declarations concerning them. This should have warned the brethren at once to be on their guard. For this is exactly what our synod of 1924 expressed! They indeed think that they have sufficiently studied and discussed the matter to declare with the clear insight of faith that there is no common grace.

How Zwier distorts matters! We must admire his dexterity. The truth is that the Christian Reformed Church, not we, established ecclesiastical dogmas concerning common grace. On the basis of those ecclesiastical declarations, they expelled us from their fellowship. While we were in the Christian Reformed Church and in the Protestant Reformed Churches, we never insisted on an ecclesiastical expression concerning common grace. Now Greydanus declares that there is an insufficiently clear insight of faith to make ecclesiastical declarations that establish the doctrine of common grace. And Zwier says, "Hocus pocus; that is exactly what our synod said. You, the Protestant Reformed people, made such declarations."

Is it not sufficient to make one dizzy?

What is the point that Zwier so dexterously distorts? It is very simple. When he accuses us of having done what Greydanus thinks should not be done, he conveniently forgets that the professor was speaking of *ecclesiastical* declarations. Zwier says that we declare that there is no common grace. We do declare this. It is my sacred conviction that the theory of common grace is a very dangerous error. I am deeply convinced that a church that adopts this error is un-Reformed and is bound to depart from the Reformed truth more and more. But this is not the issue. The issue concerns *ecclesiastical* declarations. I ask in all seriousness, "Zwier, if you will stop turning about for a moment, who made ecclesiastical declarations concerning common grace? Did we? You know better! That is exactly what your church did in the three points!"

Conclusion

Yes, Zwier says, but our synod clearly declared that it did not intend to formulate any dogma concerning common grace in *all its implications*. But that is not the issue. Not in all its implications did the synod of 1924 establish the doctrine of common grace. Had the synod attempted to do that, it would have made a strange hodgepodge of it, as is evident from what it declares now. But the synod of 1924 certainly made *ecclesiastical* declarations in which the most fundamental principles of the doctrine of common grace were established, especially those that concern the point about which Greydanus asks sundry questions. That is the issue. Also on this point Zwier does not agree with Greydanus.

Therefore Zwier must not think he has a reason to be offended when we declare that he is heaving to in order to leave the impression with the Christian Reformed reading public that he fully agrees with Greydanus. This is simply a fact, and it is so clear that it is hardly acceptable that he did not know it himself.

In conclusion, I must say a word about our rejection by the Christian Reformed Church.

We have always maintained that we did not *secede* from the Christian Reformed Church, but we were *expelled*, or *ejected*. We mean two things by this term. First, the Christian Reformed Church deposed pastors and consistories from their offices and from the fellowship of the church in spite of being well aware and declaring by synodical decision that those officebearers were soundly Reformed regarding the fundamental truths as they are formulated in the confessions, and that those officebearers did everything in their power—if it were possible with the maintenance of a good conscience regarding the Reformed truth—to remain in the fellowship of the Christian Reformed Church. Second, we mean that our depositions and expulsions took place in a very unrighteous and ungodly way.

For this reason I was surprised that Zwier had the courage to refer to this black page in the history of his denomination. He can do this only in the confidence that his readers will not consult that history, so that he only has to relate it to them and interpret it as he pleases. How does he present this matter and how does he defend his representation of the history? He writes, "An ejection did not take place in 1924. The brethren were not ejected, but they broke the bond of fellowship with our church. They tore themselves away from our denominational fellowship. It was not an ejection but a breach."

This presentation he defends by stating that ejection is the same as excommunication. He declares that excommunication is the same as what in biblical times was known as casting out of the synagogue. He reasons that we were not cut off as members, and therefore were not ejected. We leave it to Zwier's responsibility that he puts Christian discipline and excommunication on a par with casting out of the synagogue. I do not agree with him, and I maintain that although we were not excommunicated, we were nevertheless expelled, or ejected. I remark further that Zwier knows quite well that this argument has nothing to do with the issue in question, for we never alleged that we were cut off by excommunication. However, it may be said that if the Christian Reformed Church had had the power and the opportunity, they also would have excommunicated us from the church. Zwier feels that this argument does not touch the issue. He must admit that we were deposed, and that as officebearers we were expelled from the fellowship of his denomination. But having admitted this, he asks, why were they deposed? About this he writes as follows:

> The brother [Zwier refers here only to me. He forgets the consistories and the other pastors] was deposed from his office because he refused to walk in the orderly ecclesiastical way, as this is prescribed for officebearers in such cases in the Formula of Subscription. He became worthy of his deposition because of his violation of the solemn promise to act according to this Formula in the case of a doctrinal difference.

Conclusion

Zwier tells us further that in his mind that was the correct presentation of the case, but to make sure he consulted the official ecclesiastical reports.

> The classis did not demand him to declare his agreement with the declarations of the synod of Kalamazoo, but in harmony with the Formula of Subscription, he could appeal to the next synod and in the meantime refrain from making propaganda for his deviating sentiments. They had a right to ask this of him, for every officebearer solemnly promises this by his signature on the Formula of Subscription. The brother, therefore, was not deposed from his office because he disagreed with the synodical declarations of 1924. He may not say that he was rejected on the ground of his conception of the doctrine of grace.

What sophistry! It is not only Zwier's sophistry, but also that of the official reports. But who, even though he is unable to point to the untruth in this entire argument, is not convinced that I was expelled from the churches solely because of my attitude regarding the three points? No matter how badly Zwier distorts and misrepresents the matter, of this everyone remains thoroughly convinced. The deception of this entire argument lies in the appeal to the Formula of Subscription. The question is, did I really break the solemn promise I gave by my signature on the Formula? The opposite is true. I most emphatically kept my promise, and the Christian Reformed Church will corroborate the truth of this statement. What is the promise I made when I signed the Formula of Subscription? The following:

> We…do hereby sincerely and in good conscience before the Lord declare by this, our subscription, that we heartily believe and are persuaded that all the articles and points of doctrine contained in the Confession and Catechism of the Reformed Churches, together with the explanation

of some points of the aforesaid doctrine made by the National Synod of Dordrecht, 1618–19, do fully agree with the Word of God.

We promise therefore diligently to teach and faithfully to defend the aforesaid doctrine, without either directly or indirectly contradicting the same, by our public preaching or writing. We declare, moreover, that we not only reject all errors that militate against this doctrine, and particularly those which were condemned by the above mentioned synod, but that we are disposed to refute and contradict these, and to exert ourselves in keeping the church free from such errors. And if hereafter any difficulties or different sentiments respecting the aforesaid doctrines should arise in our minds, we promise that we will neither publicly nor privately propose, teach, or defend the same, either by preaching or writing, until we have first revealed such sentiments to the consistory, classis, and synod, that the same may be there examined, being ready always cheerfully to submit to the judgment of the consistory, classis, and synod, under the penalty in case of refusal to be, by that very fact, suspended from our office. (Formula of Subscription, in *Confessions and Church Order of the Protestant Reformed Churches,* 326)

This we promised, and that promise we never broke. We always have agreed heartily with the three forms of unity mentioned by name in the Formula of Subscription. By our signatures on the Formula we promised diligently to teach the doctrine contained in the three forms of unity, never to teach anything contrary to them, and to refute all errors repugnant thereto. Nothing else we promised. We have diligently accomplished everything we promised. Never did we promise to maintain and defend the declarations of the synod of the Christian Reformed Church of 1924. Since those declarations are serious errors, by our signature on the Formula we promised to oppose them. We also did that very diligently. Therefore, it is sophistry for Zwier to follow the reports of the ecclesiastical gatherings and to apply the Formula of Subscription to the three points.

If he had admitted that we should have acted according to the Formula of Subscription with regard to the three points, we would have stated our objections against some parts of the doctrine contained in the confessions. That was not the case.

Zwier will probably say this is *our* contention, but the view of the synod was that whoever cannot sign the three points is in conflict with the three forms of unity, and for that reason the case was covered by the Formula of Subscription. We reply that we have the testimony of the Christian Reformed Church to the contrary. Before its classis deposed us, its synod had already expressed itself differently in 1924, declaring that we were not in agreement with the three points. Nevertheless, "it cannot be denied that, in the basic truths of the Reformed faith as set forth in our confessions, they are Reformed, albeit with a tendency to be one-sided" (*1924 Acts of Synod of the Christian Reformed Church*, 147).

That one-sidedness was in the Reformed direction. The synod of 1924 judged that we were too strongly and strictly Reformed (*hyper-Calviniste*, as Henry Beets expressed it later). Whoever is acquainted with the condition of the Christian Reformed Church and knows of its strong Arminian tendency, which Dr. Klaas Volbeda and Dr. Y. P. de Jong readily and strongly admitted, will also understand that the judgment of one-sidedness means very little. When Christian Reformed people judge one to be one-sided, he can safely conclude that he is keeping his course right in the center of the Reformed way.

In July of 1924, the synod declared that we were Reformed in the fundamental doctrines of the confessions. The synod said that that could not be denied, which means that however eager many were at that time to deny it, and however furiously they attacked us to show that we were un-Reformed, it could not be denied. Herewith the synod declared that we had not broken our promises given by our signatures on the Formula of Subscription, although we disagreed with the three points. Therefore I appeal to that synodical testimony for the truth of the statement that my difference with the three points had nothing to do with my promise given by my signature under the Formula of Subscription, and that the classis had no right to appeal to the Formula against me. It was the duty of the classis to bring its objections to synod against the certification of being Reformed that it had given us. I conclude therefore that I diligently kept my promise.

Now a word about the term *ejected*.

By this I refer to the unjust and wicked treatment accorded me, a treatment that was so unrighteous that I was actually amazed that Zwier had the courage to refer to that history. Let me mention some of the most remarkable incidents.

The following are minor matters that I will not emphasize: The conspiracy of several leaders of the Christian Reformed Church in those days; the social gathering in Holland, Michigan, where it was said, "He must be expelled, but how can it be done? It will be impossible by means of the confessions"; and the protest against me, which had been distributed throughout the classis and to all the consistories without my being informed of it, a copy of which I found on a table in the home of the elder with whom I lodged while filling a classical appointment in East Martin in April of 1924. Nor will I emphasize the outright lies of a minister who appeared at my consistory with his protest, of which he had five hundred copies printed. He first insisted that he had not distributed the copies, but later admitted that he had about four hundred left. And I will not emphasize that one protest appeared at the May gathering of Classis Grand Rapids East as a consistory's overture, but afterward it was made known that the consistory had not adopted the protest and that it was the pastor's grievance.

Conclusion

I will point to worse things. Contrary to all rules and order, all the synodical documents that referred to my case were prepared by Classis Grand Rapids West as late as May 1924 for the June meetings of synod. I protest that at that classical meeting no one would discuss common grace with me. Classis claimed that the matter concerned the churches in common and, therefore, only synod could discuss it. I had implored the classis to appoint someone or, if classis desired, to appoint six to debate common grace with me. But all discussion was carefully avoided.

I complain that in Kalamazoo the committee of preadvice regarding the matter of common grace day after day assembled to discuss my case behind closed doors, without calling me in, without asking me one question, and without discussing a single thing with me personally.

I accuse the Christian Reformed Church because the synod of 1924 committed the wickedness of refusing me the privilege of defending myself. The rule is that one should be invited to do so; synod never invited me. The rule is that in one's case he may freely speak for as long as he desires. I was present in the auditorium of the church in Kalamazoo, but was never invited to come to the front. The first time I asked for the floor in my own case, I was refused on the ground that I had nothing to do with the matter. Yet the matter under discussion was my own case! The second time, because I realized that synod would never ask me to defend myself, I asked for the privilege of speaking just once. To persuade synod to grant me that privilege, I promised that I would not ask again! This promise they should never have accepted, but they did so very eagerly. Somewhat later when I was present at the discussion of my case and unable to refrain, I asked for the floor again and was refused. Synod reminded me of my promise not to ask again to speak in my defense! Then I left and never appeared again at the gathering of the synod. Nor did synod ever call me.

How can Zwier have the audacity to write about those things, since from the platform of the auditorium where he took minutes he was an eyewitness of what I have written about?

Did you ever hear of the notorious "robber-synod"? When I think of the Christian Reformed synod of 1924, the law of association of ideas compels me to think of that "robber-synod."

At the meeting of classis on May 21, 1924, discussion was avoided on the pretext that the matter pertained to the churches in common and therefore should be discussed only by synod. And the synod refused me the privilege of self-defense, because my own case did not concern me!

I accuse those churches because of the unrighteous treatment accorded me and my consistory by the correspondence-classis of November–December, 1924. I say correspondence-classis, for it was just that and nothing else. It was made a correspondence-classis because all public discussion was eschewed. Classis invited the theological professors to help in the case against me. The professors accepted the invitation on the condition that they would not have to appear at the classical meetings. Behind the screens, giving me no opportunity to face the classis, the professors gave their advice. There they appointed a committee that did not give a complete report to the classis, but brought it piecemeal. When a certain part of the report was delivered, my consistory was ordered to consider it and to answer in writing. The classis thereupon adjourned and my consistory obediently composed an answer. Thus the process was repeated. From the faculty and the committee through the classis the case was referred to my consistory, and from my consistory through the classis the matter was referred back to the committee and the faculty.

The classis deposed my entire consistory because, according to the official statement, it was guilty of "rebellion against the ecclesiastical authorities."

There I offered to submit to an examination of the classis to be conducted on the basis of scripture and the confessions. But classis would not. There classis suspended me, without even making any temporal provision for me, because I refused to be silent in respect to the three points.

Therefore, I maintain that we were *ejected*!

And why?

Because the Christian Reformed Church adopted the Arminian doctrine that God's grace is general.

And because we desired to maintain the truth that God's grace is always particular!

www.ingramcontent.com/pod-product-compliance
Lightning Source LLC
LaVergne TN
LVHW051828080426
835512LV00018B/2781